The
CULTURE
PURPLE

empower.ED

This book is dedicated to the hearts of all the Fathers & Mothers, as well as that of each Son & Daughter.

Table of Contents:

Section One: To the Fathers & Mothers

Section Two: Our Mission

Section Three: The Process of Purple

Section Four: You Are Valued

Section Five: You Are Loved

Section Six: You Have Purpose

Section Seven: We Believe in You

restore.HOPE

rebuild.IDENTITY

empower.PURPOSE

Section One:
To the Fathers & Mothers

A Generational Movement

Our process of hope, identity and purpose comes from an old, time-tested way of building society through a family structure where generations prepare the way into a hopeful future for one another. This "family structure" goes far beyond the walls of a family home, and can teach us to father and mother all the youth of society, impacting the future of a culture or nation by valuing that future which is presently in front of us right now. How we see that generation of youth, and at-risk youth around the world will determine what we give them.

> We don't just want to sponsor the survival of the next generation; we want to empower them to fulfill every purpose they were created for. We want to give them vision, which will give them hope. We want to give them belonging to a greater family, which will give them identity. We want to give them permission to dream, and courage to try stepping into those dreams, which will give them purpose.

Change doesn't have to come from a top down legislation from the "blue" or the "red," it can come from the ground up through a purple process and a royal generation of cross-cultural family that learns to see the best in one another, and to bring out the most. It can come from a generation not defined by age, but who are marked by coming together in a powerful form of family that extends all across the world.

The Culture Purple is a generational movement seeking to turn the hearts of the fathers and mothers towards the young arising generation (not just literal fathers & mothers), and the hearts of that arising generation towards the fathers and mothers. As a father or mother, we can empower the next generation and help them be fulfilled in their identity and purpose. We can see those struggling to survive begin to thrive and flourish. And in helping the next generation become fulfilled in their purpose for such a time as this, we too will be fulfilled in much of our own purpose.

The focus of this process is to help you empower a grassroots movement to impact and change culture wherever you are at, by rebuilding the foundation of value, love, purpose and belief within those you love and lead, and empowering one another in hope, identity and purpose.

Imagine a nation, a school or community changed because they were strengthened and empowered to be a foundational generation. Now, imagine that generation can't get there with out you, and yours. But, it's hard to give to someone else that which we have never received for ourselves. We recognize that many in the father/mother generation never had parents or others in their lives that gave them such a blessing of unconditional value, love, belonging, or belief.

Our desire is to restore hope, to rebuild identity, and to empower purpose; and we don't just want that for the next generation, we want it for you, the fathers and mothers too. We want you to be fulfilled in who you were created to be, and to know how to go and give the same to your own family, those you love and lead, or to any young person who needs it worldwide. There are foster kids, refugees, street kids and many more craving that kind of family structure and legacy—and it just might be able to happen through you and I. But first, before you think about all the good and impact you can give by taking this to others, I want you to focus on what you personally might need to receive in this way. We want to speak directly to you, too.

To the Fathers & Mothers,

For multiple generations we have had a culture of absent fathers, and even mothers too. Absent doesn't necessarily mean a single parent home, orphaned or lacking physical presence in other ways. Absent can still be true even in the presence of one another. We live in a culture driven to prove self for the sake of identity and to earn or work for value and approval. And this battle doesn't automatically go away when someone has children either. Most fathers and mothers carry their own battles, wounds and areas of lack right into that next phase of life. Many are still trying to be fulfilled by success, money, approval

10

and so much more. We have a culture starved and striving for significance, much of which can be seen every day on social media platforms everywhere.

My dad experienced his "aha moment" when he heard someone once say, "You can climb the ladder of success your whole life, only to find that it was propped up against the wrong building." He was pretty high up one of those ladders too, as many of you might be as well. But when he came down from that place he became much more fulfilled himself, and then began to create those same ladders for others, and helped direct them in the right direction. People talk all the time of the "rat race" of culture, but we don't often talk of the "why?" that keeps it going. That "why?" is that root of identity in our lives that perhaps hasn't been filled, or *fulfilled*. It keeps us climbing ladders that lead to hamster wheels, that lead to more ladders, and, well, you get the picture.

Because of this normal, accepted part of culture most fathers and mothers have had to earn or fight for whatever they've gotten in life; rarely experiencing the kind of freely given love, value, belonging and worth we're talking about with *The Culture Purple*. Most didn't have parents that were present, or that didn't know how to give such a free blessing away because they were never given such themselves.

That's where I want to start right now. If you have grown up and perhaps even raised kids or grandkids of your own, and have never had a father or mother stop their life long enough to look at you, *see you*, your heart and all the goodness and treasures inside you; if you've never had someone see the best in you and be able to speak it out over you, that's what I want to start with right now.

I want you to know that you are valued just for who you are; not for what you have or have earned, but simply because you are you. You bring your own unique goodness, life, love and presence into the room just by walking into it. You don't have to do anything, bring anything, prove anything; you just have to show up and be you. I honor you and believe in you, simply because of who you are and that you carry a special identity within that is unmatched. I am so thankful you are in this world and this world will never be the same simply because you entered it.

I also want you to know that you are loved. Too many people have grown up trying to work for love or to prove that they are love-worthy, but I am here to make sure you know that is a lie from the pit of hell, because you are loved just for who you are. The moment you came into being, no matter how adverse of situation you or your parents were in, you were, and are, *loved!* I'm sorry for the way many of us in the world have fortified the wrong kind of love in your life; please forgive us. But from here on out, I hope and pray with all my heart that you will know you are loved in the most free and powerful ways possible, that you no longer have to live *for* love, but you can live *from* love. I love you and I don't even know you! Though, I would like to.

Chances are you have worked very hard in your life in one way or another, which looks different for us all. Chances are you have worked so hard that you've never had time or freedom to realize the purpose you carry. But the truth is, no matter what has happened up until this point, you have incredible purpose in this world. You have been designed with unique purpose that is waiting to leave a mark wherever you go, whatever you grasp, just like the unique fingerprints you leave behind on whatever you touch. There is someone, somewhere in the world who is literally waiting for what you carry; whose life will be so impacted because you stepped into purpose. And I know how challenging it can be to discover your purpose in a world where it seems like your purpose just doesn't fit. You might not be able to see its end line or destination, but just start connecting the dots one step at a time and you'll find that your life paints a picture for the world that the world cannot get from anywhere else.

I cannot finish this section without telling you the same thing my dad and mom sought to make sure I knew, and that is that we believe in you! You can accomplish anything you put your heart and mind to, and there are people in your corner who—even when they don't say it out loud, or don't know how to say it—who truly believe in you. People watch you and are encouraged by your life ten times more than they ever say out loud. People think much more highly of you than they know how to communicate, which is why we compare and measure ourselves against one another so often. But that is exactly why we don't need to compare ourselves to the person on our left or right, because you have a part to play that only you can bring. You know how to play the piano or the violin or drums when everyone else around you is actually *supposed* to be playing something else— that's the beauty of an orchestra. So just keep your eyes on the conductor and play the instrument you were created to play in this world with all your heart, give life through the life in your heart and you have no idea the hope that you will shine out to so many.

As a father myself, I bless you to be who you were created to be, to fulfill every purpose formed inside you, and to go forward and multiply great things to the world all around you. *You are valued, you are loved, you have purpose, and truly, we believe in you!*

This is for you. And soon, it will be for others through you.

Sincerely,

Joey & Destiny LeTourneau

Section Two:
Our Mission

Restore Hope

There's an old truth that states: *"hope deferred makes the heart grow sick, but when the desire is fulfilled it is a tree of life."* One of the greatest areas of lack in our world is true, authentic hope. There are a lot of counterfeit forms of hope that try and lure us into their cycle of want, but no amount of those things ever fills us up or makes us content.

Conversely, I have traveled around the world and found *SO MUCH* hope hidden in what would seem like the most unlikely of places. I have met some of the most poor and hurting people living in impoverished streets who became great champions of hope right where they were.

> This tells us that circumstances do not dictate hope; rather, we dictate hope through what we see—or better yet—*how we choose to see*. There should never be a lack of hope in the world as long as you live in it; because hope doesn't come through circumstances, it is born through people.

This is where we start to restore hope. We don't just create more programs of hope or even live towards our own hopes and dreams; because we need more than the few who know how to make hope a reality in their own life. If we truly want to see foundational level hope restored in culture we choose and learn to see one another again through perspective that always searches for hope, even if it's a single glimmer of light trying to break through the dark grip of the world.

We choose to be hope for someone else. We choose to help rebuild them from the inside out. We choose to empower them into lives of powerful purpose, agents of change in their own family, community and nation. Hope will be at the forefront of lasting change, *it must be*. But it will only happen if you and I begin to extract it in its truest form from within those we love and lead; not to mention from within those the world might never expect, those who are secretly brimming with smothered hope. In a world that preys on us to find hope in success, money, popularity, power, or the new trend, we have to become a people who know how to live and empower hope from the inside out. Change a person's perspective and you'll change their whole life.

Rebuild Identity

A good portion of this material is dedicated to rebuilding identity on a personal level, and hopefully, on a corporate and cultural level. One important thing to remember with identity is that it is "Who" you are, not necessarily whom you *feel* you are. Our feelings are important and real, but they are not always truth. Sometimes we feel angry, or go through a season of hurt, but that doesn't mean that either of those are now "Who" we are. It is vital that we learn how to differentiate between who we are and what we feel, as we don't want to become a product of our feelings and/or wounds. Instead, we want to have our wounds healed, dive down past them and find the gold that has always been there; it's just been buried by the ways or opinions of the world. When we talk identity, we're talking about intrinsic value built into your created DNA, a place where you are free, whole, secure, peaceful, joyful, hopeful and back to that innocent version of you—then learning to grow, live and give *from* that place.

Empower Purpose

You have something to give the world, and we're going to talk about all different facets of that throughout this journey. We want you to be empowered in your life-giving purpose, and to help you empower others. Instead of a world that seeks to gain power for self, we get to build a world where we are so secure in our identity and worth that we freely empower others. There is such joy in helping others be fulfilled, but it's hard to feel that unless we are first walking our own journey of fulfillment. Both are important, and that is what this book is designed to lead through. We seek to empower both the Fathers and Mothers, and the Sons and Daughters of the world. Together, we will see a greater level of fulfillment of purpose, and promise.

How to Use this Guide

You can use this book personally, with your family, for a mentoring relationship, with a classroom, a youth organization, a church, a sports team, a different culture and community, or even to empower a whole generation in your nation, maybe even another nation. The goal of this guide is to help you empower yourself and others into greater hope, through identity, and towards a fulfilling purpose.

You can use this book as a training, as an informal journey, to learn and gather information, or in many others ways. You can contact us about having it translated into another language, or you can adapt some of its concepts for a younger audience that you love or lead. However you use this book, we hope it is to build and empower a young generation to fulfill their promise, and to unite multiple generations in purpose. Thank you!

Section Three:
The Process of Purple

"If you can change a person's perspective, you can change their whole life." — Unknown

Why Purple?

Purple has long been a storied color known for its association with royalty, and therefore with a royal family line. It wasn't merely chosen for this "royal" role because of its color though, but because of its process.

See, the history of purple tells us that its depth of color, vibrancy and uniqueness was not easy to come by. They didn't merely mix red and blue as we might today. Rather, they had to learn how to slowly extract it from a hidden place. Purple was, and is, a process. Here is part of purple's story as told by Wikipedia:

> *"As early as the 15th century BC the citizens of Sidon and Tyre, two cities on the coast of Ancient Phoenicia, (present day Lebanon), were producing purple dye from a sea snail called the spiny dye-murex.[23] Clothing colored with the Tyrian dye was mentioned in both the Iliadof Homer and the Aeneid of Virgil.[23] The deep, rich purple dye made from this snail became known as Tyrian purple.[24]*

The process of making the dye was long, difficult and expensive. Thousands of the tiny snails had to be found, their shells cracked, the snail removed. Mountains of empty shells have been found at the ancient sites of Sidon and Tyre. The snails were left to soak, then a tiny gland was removed and the juice extracted and put in a basin, which was placed in the sunlight. There a remarkable transformation that took place.

In the sunlight the juice turned white, then yellow-green, then green, then violet, then a red which turned darker and darker. The process had to be stopped at exactly the right time to obtain the desired color, which could range from a bright crimson to a dark purple, the color of dried blood. Then either wool, linen or silk would be dyed. The exact hue varied between crimson and violet, but it was always rich, bright and lasting.[25] Tyrian purple became the color of kings, nobles, priests and magistrates all around the Mediterranean."

> I believe that purple is still a process for us today. It's a measure of extraction, learning to extract the precious from what the world may even label as worthless.

The process of purple is us learning once again to bypass the "tyranny of the urgent," as John Maxwell labels it, to forsake social media "hot takes," and deciding to overcome the immediacies and instant gratification of today's culture to embrace an involved process of discovering and extracting the royalty hidden in people near and far, young and old, rich and poor.

Sometimes you're sitting in the presence of young kings and queens and you don't even know it.

Purple isn't about an external color we're painting the world, it is a culture we live towards our neighbor that learns to see the best, and bring out the most from within each life, and even circumstances that we meet and face every day. Purple is what I like to call an inside-out proposition—a culture we can create in our lives, our relationships, homes, offices, communities, nations and more that once again learns to search for, wait for, and mine for a true form value hidden inside every single person, a perspective and culture that we all might seek to live from once again.

When we choose to become a people who live out this "purple" culture, we'll become a growing, royal family structure that creates belonging, that breathes hope, one that offers authentic freedom and healing, and we'll be a culture that empowers purpose and dreams to be genuine, if not frequent realities—regardless of circumstance. When we learn to live purple towards one another, we'll find long hidden treasures that our world and culture is desperate for today.

I know, because I have found some of the greatest treasures in what the world would say are the most unlikely of places.

An Unlikely House of Treasure

I'll never forget the moment we pulled up to the old mudded-cement home in rural Ethiopia, about forty-five minutes outside the capital city of Addis Ababa. I was pressed up against a back window of our van wondering what my family and I were about to step into.

At the time, our family was comprised of just my wife and I, and our eldest biological daughter, Mercy, who was four. I peered over the fenced compound to what the world calls an orphanage. Our new friends and guides considered it more of a family/children's home. As I began to exit the van, murmuring curiously inside myself, I heard this still, small voice rise up from within that made me realize: *"this place is a house of treasure."*

As we filed and stumbled out of the van, the small group of "orphans" came running out their door and up to the gate to greet us. The life and joy they exuded was palatable. Their hope despite their lacking circumstances was, and still is, inspiring. That day changed our lives. We met a group of 8-12 year old kids from some of the most impoverished and difficult stories possible, yet they had a value about them that could not be measured from the outside. We could see their treasures, we only needed to learn how to extract and bring them out for the world to experience as well.

California & The Mother Lode

What is known as "The Mother Lode" region of California was the primary target of the famous California Gold Rush of the mid 1800's. It spans just five counties with an area up to a mere four miles wide and one hundred twenty miles long. It represents a defining time and monumental shift in the United States, and especially the State of California. It helped bring about the birth of what we now know as the western United States and brought an incredible reformation and even revival of sorts to society and culture because of its sweeping impact. The gold rush drew incredible amounts of people in search of such a glorious find, which led people to plant and build where they previously had not. In the small window of 1848-1852 California's population grew from 14,000 people to 223,000; an exponential growth that has left its mark on history—not just because of the gold, but because of how that gold impacted the culture of every day life.

The Gold Rush is said to have brought forth 125 million troy ounces of gold, which is worth more than $50 billion in today's financial climate.

However, what is really striking about the value extracted from California and the impact it had on people and the nation is that more than 80% of the gold within the Mother Lode region is still in the ground today. Wow!

(from the website, www.historichwy49.com)

So, what we famously know as this historic, nation altering time of discovered treasure only extracted approximately 10-20% of what was available. *How much more is still waiting to be tapped into?* And how true this is this for us today? How much of what could potentially be the greatest discovery of hope is still hidden under the surface of people all around us, ripe to be brought out to the world?

> Now, I'm not just talking about the mineral form of gold. I think we must look at how this same premise can speak to us today. Even in a culture that empowers freedom, dreams and entrepreneurship, perhaps we have only scratched the surface of what remains underneath, and all around us. How many more life altering, culture-awakening treasures are just hidden, waiting to be found and extracted from the lives all around us near and far?

My family and I had the privilege of living on the edge of this "Mother Lode" region for a time. And I can't help but wonder if we actually had these life-changing, world altering riches not far below our feet, just out of our eyes' reach. And I hope we start to wonder the same thing about the lives directly within our home, community or workplace. I hope we start to wonder how many life-changing, world-altering purposes and dreams are inside those all too familiar lives all around us; those who we may have judged as ordinary or lacking, hidden treasures inside them that are right now, in fact, just outside our eyes' reach.

If we think the 20% found of the California Gold Rush changed a nation, how much more cultural reformation will we encounter when we start to extract the precious from what we have too long called familiar, or even worthless?

This is why this "royal extraction" and empowerment process of The Culture Purple is so important: *it will teach us to see what we have missed*, and how to bring out the most from such. Let's not leave having only discovered 10-20% of what is right at our fingertips. Let's decide together that we will not let that other 80% fall to the ground to lie dormant in our families, communities or world. Let's see what that other 80% might mean to that one life you value enough to extract it from, let alone the many others that their life will no doubt impact over time.

The Culture Purple is about finding the other 80% that is still hidden in the lives, especially young lives, all around us today. That is the true mother lode. And that is our charge today!

Empowerment is Hard

There's a very natural reason why we don't often go after the other 80%, and that is because empowerment is hard—very hard sometimes! But then again, so is finding gold. It's usually found in dark, rocky, dirty, hard-to-reach places that are not comfortable or easy to persist in.

But, it's not a question of whether or not this empowerment and extraction process is easy or hard—*it's whether it is worth it.*

In today's culture we get most of our worth out of what we do, or the labels we seek for others to define us by. There is much more to cover on this cultural identity epidemic, but that's what this whole purple journey is actually all about, so more on that soon. But there is a great impact on our ability to empower one another and that's why I bring it up now. Empowerment can be a scary thing because it usually involves giving power or freedom to someone who is early in their process, someone who is likely to make a mistake along their potential-filled journey, or heaven forbid even fail. And isn't that perhaps what we are so afraid of?

We're too often afraid that their failures will be tied to or reflect negatively on what we do or our reputation. Yet, this is exactly what inhibits us, and them. *We have to let them fail*, or at least have the freedom to do so. And we have to realize that failure is often a very necessary part of true success. It has been said many times before by many people in many different ways, but the reality is this: failure is a much more reliable teacher than success.

If we want those we love and lead to learn and grow it probably has to be at our expense, not theirs. Otherwise it will be at the expense of that other 80% that is still waiting inside them.

Those we truly empower will almost certainly mess up. They will fail us. And we might fail them too. But let us not fail in being there, in giving them every chance to succeed, in offering the grace necessary to fail, learn and get back up again. They will grow much more from that process than they would a perfectly controlled result the first attempt. And isn't that the true goal anyway—***growth***?

Our culture's identity epidemic is directly connected to being such a results-oriented, measurement culture. Now, I'm not one for the "participation trophy" either, but I am one who favors a perseverance award. There is usually more value in one who learns to persevere and overcome than there is one who simply wins the first time.

> Empowerment calls for us to do right by them, certain of the other 80% inside them by spending the 20% in our life that we're living off of today. If we all learn to spend our 20% on empowering someone else's 80%, then we'll never go into debt as a people again. You might occasionally lose your 20, but someone else is using theirs to extract your 80. It's a multiplication of life and true worth.

I've had many successes and many failures in empowering others, and in being empowered myself. I promise you it can be messy. But I also can promise you that it's worth it.

Alex

I first met Alex on a vision trip to Ethiopia before my family and I moved to live there. Our primary contact in country was driving us around, answering all our questions while giving us a taste of the culture. She kept telling us about this one young man she'd known since he was little, Alex. He had been away from the capital city of Addis Ababa for some time now, ever since he got out of prison. He was in his early twenties and a couple years before had been falsely accused, taking the wrap for something a group of his friends had done—though he had put himself in the wrong place with the wrong people.

She wished we could meet him, and so did we. So much of our hope in Ethiopia was to mentor at-risk youth and raise up local young leaders to be those who brought change to their communities and nation. When I started to hear about Alex my spirit leapt. If only I could have the chance to connect with him, but last he had been heard from by our contact he was hours away down country and not easy to get a hold of.

Then, we were on one of our drives through the city amidst hundreds of the usual passers by over the medians and around the streets when our contact stopped suddenly, rolled down her window and burst out with a yell, *"Alex!"*

He had just come back into the city that week we happened to be there. And here was our chance encounter on the streets in the middle of this huge, international city. I had only a brief interaction with him at first, but I could see what was within him, knowing he was different and believing he had more to offer than he knew.

See, Alex had grown up on the streets alone, living in a plastic house since he was seven years old. His dad died when he was two and five years later when his mom re-married, her new husband (as was fairly customary at the time) expected her to relinquish her kids and start anew with him. His story rocked me to my core and made my heart well up with tears. Thankfully, it was only the beginning and we were about to get to play a big part in his redemption story, and he in ours.

I knew with all of me that Alex was our link to the streets, as Ethiopia—Addis Ababa in particular—was home to an inordinate amount of street kids and orphans. But first, we wanted Alex to see himself in a new way—through value, through love, through purpose, and belief.

(Alex with one of the groups of kids on the streets that he began to "father.")

Besides the eight young orphans at the rural home, Alex was the first we met there that we felt compelled to go after that 80% treasure still buried within his life. We didn't call it The Culture Purple back then, but that's what it was. Some months later we moved our family to Addis Ababa with my wife Destiny, who was four months pregnant, our daughter, Mercy, and as many suitcases full of our life that they'd allow us to fit on the plane. I knew one thing for sure upon our arrival to our new home; Alex was our priority, not programs or any other big plans, just Alex—and of course those eight precious, powerful little lives at the orphanage home.

Sure and unsure at the same time, we invited Alex to move into our new home with us to stay in a room at the back of our compound. It was a huge unknown, challenging at many turns, and also one of the best decisions we ever made.

Alex became family—that was one of the biggest keys to empowering him. He needed to belong.

I started mentoring Alex every day, and in turn he would show me/us around the streets of Addis Ababa and help us connect with the people and culture. We'd walk miles and miles each day through some of the most impoverished streets, meeting both broken and amazing lives, learning how to love and empower them together. We found so much hidden hope on those streets.

My family and I could go on for hours with stories about Alex, and he will pop up more from time to time in this journey—as it wouldn't be possible without him. But for now I want to share just one high risk/high reward "trust" story that both scared us and at the same time set everything in motion to see a movement of family and empowerment hit some of the most lowly streets not just in Ethiopia, but the world.

Trust

Trust is a big part of empowerment, and it was a slippery slope we had to climb with Alex as well. Was Alex completely trustworthy? We weren't sure yet. He proved that he was, but not all will be. However, we usually have to give trust away to someone once or twice before we know what they will do with it. And even if they let us down, it's worth it. Why? Because we can't get close to that 80% of hidden treasures without trust helping to pioneer the way. If we could, everyone would do it and all the gold—real and figurative— would already be found.

Starting over, we had very little in our home furniture wise and were living on a meager budget. We didn't know Alex well. We'd spent some time with him on our pre-move trips, mentored him upon arriving and now he had lived with us only a couple weeks. But our times walking the streets let me see how he handled even small things with integrity. We had about two hundred dollars left for our family until we had another form of provision came our way. It wasn't a lot but if we were careful we could use it wisely on groceries and transport until our next provision arrived. But then one day my wife and I both felt compelled to take another leap of faith in empowering Alex. It wasn't a leap we were comfortable with per se, but we both knew that, despite our very rational questions, we were supposed to go through with it.

We felt this need to give Alex all the money our family had left, in cash, no strings attached. Insane, right?! We kind of thought so too. We had questions about what we would do for food, etc. the next two weeks, and to be honest we had big questions about how all of that money, all at once, might even affect Alex negatively. Coming from the streets with nothing, two hundred dollars cash could be like winning the lottery, something that breaks a lot of people. Alex was doing so well and we didn't want to give him too much freedom too quickly. But, we also felt led to put our faith in Alex, to go all-in on him, take part of the 20% we had left and invest it in going after the 80% within him.

So, one night we went and grabbed all our cash, called Alex into the kitchen and said,

"We're supposed to give this to you. No strings attached. We love you unconditionally and we believe in you. Use it how you see best."

I'll never forget those moments that followed. Alex didn't jump up and down like he won the lottery, in fact, he barely even smiled. Instead, the love and belief we put inside him by putting that money in his hands made him tremble under the responsibility he suddenly felt entrusted with. It broke him, but not in a bad way. He had never been trusted so freely before, without condition.

And that trust empowered him to see the money or the opportunity in a very different way.

Over the next two weeks Alex primarily did two things with all that cash. First, he went to the bank and asked them to break it into single bills (which was thousands of the local "birr" currency). Then, he took the rest of the money and bought groceries and other household needs for our family and home—which he was now a part of—to help make it through the next couple weeks.

I'll never forget the way Alex trembled in such a healthy way after being entrusted with so much responsibility. He felt the love and belief. Then, he took those single bills out every day and found purpose in valuing others who had grown up like him. And wouldn't you know it, the love and value he gave away to so many people on the streets started to form something of a interconnected family—kids on the streets who called on him and looked to him like a dad—something Alex himself had never really had either. That investment—and trust—that went into empowering Alex was the very thing that helped him find his purpose, and his purpose became our link to giving something very similar to hundreds more kids on the streets of Addis Ababa, Ethiopia.

Now, I don't share this story so that you'll go and recklessly give away your trust to empower someone. However, I do hope it helps you see a seed of possibility when one comes your way, and why we should be looking for those perhaps "unlikely" people or counter-intuitive opportunities around us that beckon us to see beyond fear or results and freely invest our trust in their lives. You never know when one big, unconditional seed might birth a tree that bears a whole lot of fruit.

Still today, more than ten years later, Alex's tree is still bearing fruit for many across the streets of Addis Ababa.

Why (By: NF)

The following are lyrics from a song I have used in classrooms with students. It's a deep, eloquent, vulnerable depiction on identity, and therefore of why this purple process is so important. To remember this battle reminds us why someone's value, love, purpose and belief needs to be validated and given from the inside, out. I'll let the popular artist, **NF**, take it from here as he knows this cultural, internal battle of identity very well:

"Too many faces, too many faces, too many faces

Yeah, what's the definition of success?
I don't trust the thoughts inside my head
I don't trust this thing that beats inside my chest
Who I am and who I wanna be can not connect; why?
Don't think I deserve it? You get no respect
I just made a couple mil', still not impressed
Let You Down goes triple platinum, yeah, okay, okay, I guess
Smile for a moment then these questions startin' to fill my head, not again!
I push away the people that I love the most; why?
I don't want no one to know I'm vulnerable; why?
That makes me feel weak and so uncomfortable; why?
Stop askin' me questions, I just wanna feel alive
Until I die—this isn't Nate's flow
Just let me rhyme; I'm in disguise

I'm a busy person, got not time for lies; one of a kind
They don't see it; I pull out they eyes; I'm on the rise!
I've been doin' this for most of my life with no advice
Take my chances, I just roll the dice, do what I like
As a kid, I was afraid of heights, put that aside

Now I'm here and they look so surprised, well so am I, woo!
They don't invite me to the parties but I still arrive
Kick down the door and then I go inside
Give off that "I do not belong here" vibe

Then take the keys right off the counter, let's go for a ride
Why do y'all look mortified?
I keep to myself, they think I'm sorta shy, organized

Let You Down's the only song you've heard of? Well then you're behind
Story time; wish that I could think like Big Sean does, but I just can't decide

I, I don't care what anybody else thinks—lies
I do not need nobody to help me—lies
I kinda feel guilty 'cause I'm wealthy; why?
I don't understand, it's got me questioning like, "Why?"
Just tell me why—now back to this flow

Inside I feel divided
Back when I ain't had a dime, but had the drive
Back before I ever signed, I questioned life, like, "Who am I, man?" Woo!"
Nothin' to me's ever good enough
I could be workin' for twenty-four hours a day and think I never did enough
My life is a movie but there ain't no tellin' what you're gonna see in my cinema
I wanna be great but I get it in the way of myself and I think about everything that I could never be

Why do I do it though? Ayy, yeah
Why you always lookin' aggravated?
Not a choice, you know I had to make it
When they talk about the greatest, the gon' probably never put us in the conversation
Like somethin' then I gotta take it
Write somethin' then I might erase it
I love it, then I really hate it
What's the problem, Nathan? I don't know!

I know I like to preach to always be yourself
But my emotions make me feel like I am someone else
Me and my pride had made a pact that we don't need no help
Which feels like I'm at war inside myself but I forgot the shells
I hold my issues up for all to see, like show and tell
A lot of people know me, but, not a lot know me well
Hold my issues up for all to see, like show and tell
A lot of people know me, but, they don't know me well

Too many faces, too many faces, too many faces."

The "Why" of "Why"

"Too many faces, too many faces, too many faces..."

It is really powerful of NF to let us in on the reality that it isn't just us, but that he too battles putting on too many different faces, masks that are not authentic to who he really is. This is incredibly common for us all to different extents, and yet it isn't something we openly address very often. For a public figure to bring this to the light should help us be vulnerable to be honest with ourselves as well. How are we putting on different faces for different people? How does that impact, or even hurt us? Can we learn to be secure in who we are, just for who we are?

"Yeah, what's the definition of success?
I don't trust the thoughts inside my head
I don't trust this thing that beats inside my chest
Who I am and who I wanna be can not connect; why?"

I have a very different measurement for success than most of society as I believe it should be measured from the inside, out. Many will say that, but honestly, how many of us truly apply that consistently? Could we? What if we did? Would it be easier to trust the thoughts in our head, to trust our heart, if we allowed ourselves the freedom to put down our masks, stop trying to earn love and approval, and freely be who we were designed to be? We're often trying so hard to be something or prove something because our measure of success is so externally based, yet we are starving on the inside to be valued for who we already are.

"Don't think I deserve it? You get no respect
I just made a couple mil', still not impressed
Let You Down goes triple platinum, yeah, okay, okay, I guess..."

NF goes on to prove his previous point, letting us know that even making millions and going triple platinum with his album still didn't fill the void. I love that he openly recognizes how fleeting those external measurements, and achievements really are. He openly wants something more, and how powerful to let others in on that reality. Truth be told, we all want something more. We just haven't all learned to admit such...yet.

"I push away the people that I love the most; why?
I don't want no one to know I'm vulnerable; why?
That makes me feel weak and so uncomfortable; why?
Stop askin' me questions, I just wanna feel alive
Until I die—this isn't Nate's flow
Just let me rhyme; I'm in disguise..."

Rejection. That's the fear right there that is more prevalent than the common cold. I have to put on a mask, I push away the people I truly love, and those whom I want to be loved by; I can't be vulnerable, all because I'm afraid of being rejected. Yet, I also want to feel the freedom of not feeling or fearing that rejection. I want to get past the protections of my disguises. We want other to make us feel free. But the reality is that no one else can make us free until we decide it for ourselves first. But we can help one another be secure in that belief.

"I, I don't care what anybody else thinks—lies
I do not need nobody to help me—lies."

It's interesting, often, those who are most outspoken about not caring what anyone else thinks are usually those who care the most. And it's hard to allow people to help us if we are we're still trying so hard to earn approval and prove ourselves. See, we truly want to know that people love us and care about us for who we are, not just what we do. Yet we shoot ourselves in the foot of receiving that when we spend most of our time trying to prove we're worthy because then we don't often give them a chance to show us that unconditionally.

"Just tell me why—now back to this flow
Inside I feel divided
Back when I ain't had a dime, but had the drive
Back before I ever signed, I questioned life, like, "Who am I, man?"
Woo!"
Nothin' to me's ever good enough
I could be workin' for twenty-four hours a day and think I never did
enough
My life is a movie but there ain't no tellin' what you're gonna see in my
cinema
I wanna be great but I get it in the way of myself and I think about
everything that I could never be
Why do I do it though? Ayy, yeah..."

This battle over identity that we keep discussing, the battle between who I am and what I show you, the battle between receiving love vs. earning it; this is the battle that is at the root of the divide inside us. Often, we're still trying to prove our value to ourselves, not just to others, and if nothing is ever good enough for how I measure myself, how will I ever feel good enough for someone else?

Self-doubt, poverty of spirit, self-condemnation, these are unseen enemies that we all face. They are the internal battle that divides us and tries to conquer us. At best, many will see this battle go back and forth, win some and lose some throughout their lives. But, you have the opportunity to win this battle once and for all, to realize the value you were innately created with and live from that value for the rest of your life. No one will do it for you, you have to choose it and believe it consistently as your foundation.

"I know I like to preach to always be yourself
But my emotions make me feel like I am someone else
Me and my pride had made a pact that we don't need no help
Which feels like I'm at war inside myself but I forgot the shells."

I believe you can win this war. And then, you can help others win theirs too. We can have our pride, or we can have our true, created identity. It is us who choose which one we prioritize, and which one we live from.

This is the battle that this *Culture Purple* seeks to heal and empower you through. We want to teach you to create a culture inside yourself and others that extracts the hidden gold and true worth to be your mindset, your measurement, and the foundation you live from. You don't need to put on other faces for the world when you learn to live and give your incredible value from the inside, out. The Culture Purple is how we help one another live that out.

Section Four:
You Are Valued

"Nowadays people know the price of everything and the value of nothing." – Oscar Wilde

> ### The Culture Purple has four core values:
>
> You are VALUED.
> You are LOVED.
> You have PURPOSE.
> We BELIEVE in you!

We live in a society where, as individuals, we are typically living *for* these principles. Our hope, or goal, is for us as a culture to learn to live *from* these principles. That begins with you and I, and those we love and lead.

- You are valued for who you are, not for what you do or do not have.
- You are loved for who you are, not for what you do. You are family. You belong, unconditionally.
- You have a special, unique purpose already inside of you, waiting for you to connect the dots and see the picture of true purpose that has always been planted and growing inside you.
- You are worth believing in, and so are the people around you. All of us are fueled exponentially more when we know that there is someone who believes in us. Belief itself is a world-changer for us all.

These Four Core Values are the essence of The Culture Purple.

- First, these values become something that we believe.
- Next, they become something that we personally receive.
- Then, these four principles become something that we start to live from in our lives.
- And finally, they become what we give to others who we are guiding and empowering.

These values are at the core of how we transform culture, because first we have to let them transform our life or someone else's. They are simple but powerful principles that we have become familiar with to the point of taking them for granted; yet we don't have a secure foundation to build culture or healthy community upon without them. Our culture has become too comfortable with a value system that measures us down rather than one that innately builds us up, from the inside, out. What we need is a revived value system.

Value System

Chances are that at some point in life, probably more often than you'd like, you have felt unfairly judged. And just as likely is that the youth you raise, mentor or who surround you all feel the same way. We've all been judged unfairly, and none of us like to be the victim of such.

- Have you ever felt unfairly judged? When?
- How did this make you feel?
- In what way did the person/people measure you unfairly, and why was this unjust?

What are some of the externals we often judge others or ourselves by? How do these perhaps aid in creating unfair judgments?

- Money
- Job
- Clothes/shoes
- Family/friends

- Social status
- Grades
- Beauty/looks
- Our past
- Social media

Are those aspects of life an accurate measurement of "Who" you really are? Why or why not?

Do you like being judged negatively or unfairly by those externals? Why or why not?

None of us like to be judged or labeled negatively or unfairly by those parts of our lives. However, what I find interesting—and important—is that chances are we don't mind when someone looks at one or more of those aspects of our lives and judges us in a positive way according to those same externals.

But, if we don't like or believe in negative judgments of who we are according to these types of externals, why would we allow those same types of measurements to define our identity or worth simply because they are being judged positively at that particular time in our life? Just because it's a positive result this time, does it make it an accurate gauge of value or worth? No. It's the same type of measurement, only now, we like the results.

> What this should tell us is that one of the biggest contributors to lack of identity or hope in our lives comes not just from "what" we judge, but "how" we measure. We have learned to accept a wrong value system to measure others and ourselves by; a system of externals that whether positive or negative are still not the right scale to discover true value.

We can't just keep the positive results to determine our value and throw out the negative, or vice versa. We will never get rid of unfair judgments this way.

We have to change the means of *how* we measure value.

We shouldn't simply try and change the surface of what we are being judged or measured by; rather, we must learn to change how we are measuring. It's very important that we all learn the difference, and then learn to show that difference to those we love and lead.

The kind of value or measurement system that produces unfair judgments comes from one that measures outside-in, rather than inside-out. We will never be able to fully transform the identity epidemic in our culture unless we flip our value system inside out. This requires us to look first at intrinsic value (natural, internal) rather that produced value.

"What lies behind us and what lies ahead of us are tiny matters compared to what lives in us." - Henry David Thoreau

The Gold Standard, Standard

I find that this transition in our value system as it relates to identity is a lot like the comparison of money vs. gold. Money is like the externals that we use to measure others or ourselves by; it is paper that can be manufactured, burned up, torn, and it has no natural value of its own.

What we should be learning to measure our identity and worth by is gold. Gold doesn't just burn up, and it cannot be torn in two. It doesn't need paper money to give it worth because it already has intrinsic value.

Also, you typically look for money in a much different way than you do for gold. Money is something you have to work for or earn; something that man creates. But gold is a natural resource in creation, something that is hidden and has to be intentionally searched or mined for.

Gold often sets the standard of value for money, not the other way around. Money in our economy used to be supported by a gold standard. Gold is recognized around the world for its natural, internal, created value that it carries inside. Even when gold is covered up and hidden by different rocky, dirty surfaces—waiting to be discovered—it is still always gold!

Likewise, you are always gold. You always have your created identity inside of you. Identity is not man created, but is the output of a natural DNA within you. Neither you, nor others need to search for identity on the outside or try to measure up or react to the judgments of others. Instead, you need to discover the value you have always had on the inside and who you were created to be, bring it to the outside—and help others do the same.

On the inside you have gold that is waiting to be found, valued, and used in the world. You were created with it. We usually don't recognize our gold because we are so busy and focused looking for counterfeit forms of identity, worth and value—seeking the world's approval rather than living from the gold standard that is already inside us. Instead, let's change our value system one person at a time by learning to see others and ourselves correctly. Many of us have been trying to create man-made worth when you already have a greater form of value ready to lend itself to the world. Why should we be so far in debt to the world from trying to measure up just because we are constantly borrowing from its value system?

You or those you're empowering could literally change the world simply by deciding to flip the scales of how you value something. We could stop borrowing from the world and start lending something far greater.

From "Debt" to Making A Difference

Looking back to the eight "orphans" in that rural, Ethiopian house of treasure reminds me of how such a change happens in us, and then how it happens through us.

The eight kids in this home were always more than orphans, but that's not how the world labels them. To the world, they're basically in debt, trying to survive external and internal forms of poverty. But no matter what they didn't have, they always had value inside as well as something to give. They just needed to see and believe that such was the truth. That's where our focus was; helping them see the 80% under their surface instead of the 20% above ground that had been stolen or hurt by the world.

Week after week we spent time with the kids, focusing on just getting to know them more than putting them through our program or agenda. We needed to learn to see each of their internal treasures well enough to point them out to them. If we didn't take the time to see them, they probably wouldn't either.

Often it's our time or focus invested in something that makes it larger or more valuable. We couldn't just teach them, we had to invest in them like our own kids.

Eventually, through several progressive steps we began to call out the good, the gold, and the treasures we saw inside them. We had to speak them out, make them real and valuable. Our investment and even our words help prove someone or something's worth. The more we did this with the kids the more they began to step forward and even speak into one another's life in such a way.

These "orphans" were changing before our eyes. But really, they were just becoming who they always were. The world's monetary value system called them poor and orphans. But the gold standard within them gave them an account to start to live and give from once they believed.

Before we knew it, these special eight were helping Alex and us reach more kids just like them who were living on the streets.

They were leaders. I'll never forget when we had them all over to our house for a full weekend—the second weekend of its kind—and asked them to join us in a brainstorming session. We asked them, *"If this new perspective you've learned to see yourself in is true, is it also true for the many, many kids like you in age and circumstance who are living just outside on the streets?"* We encouraged them to go off by themselves to take some time to ponder the question, and gave them pencils and paper to write down what they thought.

I've always enjoyed having brainstorming whiteboard sessions with established or emerging leaders. But this one was the best one I've ever been a part of.

To hear the ideas coming out of their eight to thirteen year old little mouths, ideas of how to speak value, love, purpose and belief into even less fortunate kids on the streets; I was floored. We watched these kids who the world's value system labeled as "just orphans" as they defied such a measurement and learned to live *and give* from the inside-out. They took the gold they were starting to find in themselves and they started making a difference across the streets of Addis Ababa, sharing their stories through Alex and through us to many more kids who also learned that they too were truly valuable. These special eight kids weren't orphans anymore; they were world-changers who had defied the world's value system.

Thieves of Our Gold

"Comparison is the thief of joy." - *Theodore Roosevelt*

Unfortunately, we live in a world where culture is trying to steal our gold, our hidden 80%, or simply stealing our attention from recognizing where the true value is hidden in regards to our lives and identity. But how?

- The world wants to make you insecure and fearful about what you are not, so that you don't recognize and appreciate who you are.

- If the world can make you judge yourself incorrectly, then you are much more likely to judge others incorrectly as well. Then, this kind of insecurity and judgment spreads like a plague from person to person.

- When we are afraid of not measuring up to the "world's view" of us, we seek counterfeit forms of value or identity to try and prove our worth, rather than living from the true, unique worth we already have.

- When this insecurity replaces our identity, we fall into the trap of pursuing a "money" form of identity instead of living from our "gold." We protect our 20% instead of going after the other 80%. (*For clarity, we are not speaking against money itself. We are using the concept of paper "money" as a metaphor to show how it is a lesser form of value than gold.*)

- Before we know it we have a domino effect throughout culture—a world full of people who are all pursuing a false identity when so much more value waits dormant in them, and in the person next to them.

Comparison as a Thief

This is the process of how "comparison" becomes the "thief of joy." Let me paint you a picture:

You are a special part of a world-class orchestra. You're dressed up, and you take your seat behind *your* specific, important instrument. As the conductor begins your eyes are on him, but almost immediately you hear the person and instrument next to you playing a different sound and different notes of the song. Now, you're worried that either you're doing something wrong, or that the person next to you has something better. Your eyes are no longer on the conductor, but those to your right and your left. You've stopped playing your sound, and have left your part of the music. The orchestra is now missing a vital component: you and your instrument, all because you began to compare yourself rather than freely play your unique part to the best of your ability. But it doesn't have to be this way.

**COMPARISON
IS THE THIEF
OF JOY.**

Theodore Roosevelt

When we compare ourselves to others, we are looking for a worldly standard to measure up to rather than living the unique gold standard that is within us. You play a different instrument than the people on your right, and your left, and you play completely different notes of the melody. Your part is important. The unique ability to play this instrument and the sound you release from it will not play itself; it is stored up inside you. You need only to keep your eyes on the conductor, on your part of the music and freely play out loud to help make the song into what many are waiting to hear.

There is a special joy in learning to freely live out your unique, created value; a joy that insecurity and comparison want to snuff out. Fear and insecurity don't want you to see who you are, or all that you already have. Because if you do, you are much more likely to set others free to live their true value as well, and fear and insecurity will lose their way too comfortable place in society.

Learning to See the Gold

"It's not what you look at that matters, but what you see."
- Henry David Thoreau

Remember, vision is not just about seeing further. Vision is about seeing what is missed by much of the world.

To see the gold in yourself or another, you must see with different eyes and measure with a different value system. By measuring others/yourself through a different value system you will see what you couldn't see before, which means you can discover and celebrate gold that you didn't know was there before. Imagine being on a treasure hunt but being so focused on finding money that while you strive and search for dollars you are walking past piles of gold the whole time.

Your true identity, which is where your gold is at, is like an intangible version of your DNA. Neither one can be measured by the external eye alone. To be identified, both DNA and identity require someone to measure at a deeper, trained, incomparable level.

What is DNA? Why can't DNA be measured by sight alone, and how is it measured?

DNA's special mark within us is identified in things such as our fingerprints, our saliva, by our teeth, or inside a sample of hair. DNA is measured by components inside that are unique to us that we cannot fake or create on our own.

Why can't identity be measured by sight alone? What is incomparable about both our DNA and our identity?

DNA is something we all are created with, special marks inside us that are unique only to us. No one has your exact DNA, and it cannot be counterfeited. Identity is very similar.

Just as you put your fingerprint on something you touch, so too does your identity have the ability to leave its mark on the world wherever you go.

Your identity was created in you specifically, and like your DNA, no one else has an identity that matches yours exactly. You may find some people who share some similar attributes, but who are still different in many other ways. What this tells us is this: YOU ARE SPECIAL!! Truly, you are one of a kind. It is quite the opposite of comparison, and that is where you will find the true gold and the real value that you bring to the world.

As we tell stories of the amazing things that took place with the "orphans" and "street kids" in Ethiopia, one of the two major differences and contributing factors to their change was not what many expect in regards to working with young, impoverished kids.

We took care of the kids and helped with their physical needs such as food, shelter and clothing—but that was not what made the biggest difference! The #2 thing that we gave the kids (we'll discuss more of #1 later) was *vision*.

"Vision" is usually reserved for those we call visionaries, entrepreneurs, or different forms of leaders. However, if we truly believe that each person can be a leader in their own unique way, it means that vision is essential no matter what your occupation or position.

> See, if these young, hurting, impoverished kids looked at themselves with just their eyes they would see that they have little or nothing in their hands or circumstances. But when you teach them to have vision, they can look deeper within themselves and others and recognize the value that's already inside them—the value that has been there with them in their identity since birth.

There is not just one form of poverty. Physical poverty is very real and is obviously such a tough battle. However, it's not the only kind.

There is an internal poverty of spirit that goes after our true value, that which robs vision and hope, a kind of poverty that tries to keep us living the cycles of insecurity and comparison.

When we give someone vision, we give them access to start to search out that other 80% of value that's been buried within them the whole time. And once they find it they'll know how to help extract it from within others as well. No longer will they be in poverty externally or internally, they will be multipliers. That's why vision is such a vital element of empowerment, and a key ingredient of change.

It shows us where the value is and allows us to live from that place and towards dreams and purposes we would have otherwise never thought possible.

Section Five:
You Are Loved

"I sustain myself with the love of family." - Maya Angelou

The necessary truth of being unconditionally loved is yet another core section that our identity is rooted in. It's very difficult to know "who" you are when someone still believes that love comes from what they do. What we do, our deeds, are incredibly important and we'll see that come to life even more in the "Purpose" section. However, "what we do" will always be much more powerful and full of potent, world-altering impact when it flows first and foremost out of "who we are."

This section is fundamentally about learning to love or be loved for who we are first— allowing this to become a strong foundation in our lives. Truly, to live *from* love instead of *for* love has become counter cultural in our world. It seems like a simple flip by its language, but it has become deeply embedded in culture to work for or prove our love, and likewise to sometimes unknowingly require those close to us to do the same.

Nice to Meet You

This may sound silly, but one of the simplest places to recognize our culture's natural emphasis on "What we do" vs. "Who we are" is by looking at our ingrained response to meeting someone.

"Hi, I'm (insert your name here), nice to meet you."

Continue to exchange names.

"So, what do you do?"

Other than asking someone's name at a surface level, we almost automatically go next to asking someone what it is that they *do*. I've tried to adjust this habit in my own life, and it's not as easy as you might think.

I've tried to ask other basic (and some not so basic) questions first, such as: *"Where are you from? What are you interested in? What's your background? What are you passionate about? Tell me about yourself."*

Now, this could seem simple, and even silly. I'm not trying to over measure our greetings for errors in identity. However, I do think it's one small thing that can show our tendencies towards our cultural misinterpretation of identity, tendencies that are also deeply embedded in much more important parts of life, and especially in important relationships.

"Dr. Seuss-Like" Identity

I'm sure you're wondering what in the world Dr. Seuss could have to do with love and identity, other than a simple lesson hidden in one of his children's books. I was actually working on my own children's book on identity, an ode to Dr. Seuss in its unique style and language when I came up with my own chorus for this teaching:

"It's when our 'Be' and our 'Who' overtake our 'What' and our 'Do;' that is when our unhealthy fear goes away and we're now free to say, 'I'll be exactly who I was created to be.'"

As we talked about in the last section on value, insecurity is something that robs us all in different ways, at different levels and during different times in our lives. Insecurity is an unhealthy fear. *BUT*, when we prioritize loving others and being loved for who we are, it helps set us free from those kind of insecurities and performance mindsets. No longer are we trying to protect ourselves and at the same time trying to live with purpose, as it's very hard to do both at the same time. One is offensive in nature, and the other defensive. It's hard to go forward, and especially to take that first leap when you don't have secure ground under your feet—or even more so, secure ground under your heart.

THE CULTURE PURPLE

YOU are VALUED ↵
YOU are LOVED ↵
YOU have PURPOSE ↵
WE BELIEVE IN YOU!

49

Who You Are Makes a Difference

Valuing yourself for who you are or helping others do the same, as simple as that sounds, can be a very difficult process. "Who we are" is more intangible by nature, which is why we typically focus on what we do, which is usually a much more tangible measurement.

Here are some cues that can help us begin to recognize how our "who" can make such an impact vs. just living out of our "do."

Intangible Becomes Tangible:

- *When you walk into a room, WHO are you?*

- *Most people think this means, "When you walk into a room, what do you do?" But this isn't true.*

- *We typically believe that when we walk into a room we have to do something or perform something in order to get noticed or to make a difference.*

- *But, did you know that when you are living according to the right value system—from the gold inside of you—that you change a room simply by walking into it and being you?*

- *I often remind my wife of this principle. It's too easy to forget that just by "being herself" and not comparing or trying to measure up to others, that she carries a bright light that lights up every room she walks into simply by walking into it. She doesn't have to "do" anything to make that light shine; it's a natural part of her. She just has to be free to let it shine! We all do.*

- *This isn't because she can't or shouldn't do good things to help others, it's that she recognizes that what she does may impact people and the world, but not nearly as much as who she is does. For example, she may think she needs to bake something for a party in order to prove her worth. Doing/serving is a good thing, but not the best thing. The party will be much more impacted by the light she carries than the cake that she bakes. When we realize this we can do both, but prioritize the first.*

- Or, put it this way. She might think what people want most is the tangible cake that she brings. But what people would miss the most is the light she carries. We don't realize this because people often show or tell their appreciation for what we do, but they are truly impacted by who we are in their lives. We just don't tell people this often enough.

- If we focus first or only on what we do, we usually lose our identity because we're working by the world's value system. But when we learn to freely be who we were created to be, we carry intangible forms of hope without lifting a finger, and then get to add our other efforts, gifts and talents on top of that too.

We all have different intangible qualities like that inside us that come with us wherever we go. Perhaps you naturally carry peace with you, or maybe people feel "safe" when you are around because they know they can trust you. Some people carry a very warm heart about them that brings warmth to others. These are intangible qualities that leave a mark on people and places, often without you ever knowing.

- Many of us don't recognize these intangibles we carry because they aren't easily measured or "seen," yet they are part of "who" we are. They are a different part of us that makes a difference in the world—when we allow it to!

- Unfortunately, many of us cover up these intangibles in order to focus on what we can "do" or perform for others. We still need to "do" good works as well, but they should flow from who we are, not at the expense of who we are.

- It's important we accept ourselves for these intangibles that we carry, and recognize that they have as much, if not more impact than anything we can do for others. The world needs you to brighten it, warm it with your heart, bring it peace, protection, and so much more! It's already in you.

Your Difference makes a Difference. The insecurities we often try to hide away are often the lights that will shine brightest—if we let them!

That is why it is so vital that we take a core value statement such as, "You are Loved" beyond the familiar words that we know and make them into a true, believed foundation in our lives, and then help create the same for the lives all around us. It is this kind of love that becomes a platform for who we are to begin to flourish. This is beyond inclusion, acceptance or equality, it is being loved for who you are (and loving yourself) at your core regardless of what externals you're operating in. This love doesn't approve all behaviors or emotions, but it does approve you just for being you and it empowers many of your intangible, innate gifts to shine forth.

Belonging

I mentioned in the last section how there were two main ways we empowered the orphans and street kids that went beyond basic physical needs. We talked about #2 being "Vision," and how that changed the youth's perspective of their value and what they had to offer the world, let alone those in their immediate sphere of influence.

The #1 thing we saw impact and change their lives was when we found ways to show each person "Belonging."

Ultimately, it was about communicating and then showing even a child living in a plastic house on the street that he or she belongs to a family bigger than their blood, greater than their circumstances—a family by whom they felt seen, known and unconditionally loved.

It didn't happen overnight, it never does. Such love is a pattern of action that says "I don't need anything *from* you," and "nothing you do or don't do can make me love you any less." It is showing them they have their own unique place in the family just because of who they are.

A great example of this is if or when you ever go on a service project trip to an impoverished area. Usually a group will go with a need in mind and a plan or agenda of how to fix that need for the local people. This is a tremendous thing on so many levels. However, I've been on enough of these myself to learn that there is something more waiting for both parties during such a project or trip.

My team and I might build a house or structure that the local people badly need, one that they are truly grateful for. It's where we would probably invest 80-90% of our time and energy on such a trip. But, what I have always found to be funny is that by the end of the trip I'm not so taken back by what I built or the agenda I accomplished. Usually, it was one or two relationships I built during that 10-20% down time that marked my life in a way I'll never forget. And I would venture it is almost always the same for the locals on the ground. They love the building you built. They will use the water system as long as it lasts and it will literally save lives.

Yet, the thing they will remember most are those few moments when you put your arm around them, connected freely and with out agenda, and made them feel like they belong to a love that's bigger than they've ever previously known.

I've always wondered, what if we flipped it? What if we spent 70% of our trip creating belonging and new family-like relationships? What if we prioritized a "family structure" over a physical one, making that our Major and what we do for them our Minor? These relationship moments of family-like love and belonging are bi-products on most trips, yet they still bear the most fruit. We still need to go build, and serve, but let us do so out of a renewed emphasis on creating belonging and family through unconditional love.

This doesn't just apply to a service project in an impoverished area. This applies to our very own home and family. It applies to our workplace. It applies to those we teach, coach or mentor.

This is us learning to let our "be" and our "who" overtake our "what" and our "do," it is helping clean out those insecure, unhealthy fears from those all around us simply by making sure they know they are loved first, without condition. If we will create these spaces in our lives and relationships, we will see a multiplying effect that naturally empowers people to carry out great purpose from the foundation of being wholly, truly loved.

That Special House

Was there ever a house in your neighborhood growing up (doesn't have to be your house) where you and everyone else always wanted to be? Was there a place where the lights were always on, the door was always open, the table was full and you could go into the fridge anytime you wanted?

Was there one of those family homes where you always felt free, like the best and truest version of yourself—like you belonged?

I believe this is what our world needs more of, and it isn't relegated just to homes either. We can make our classrooms this way, our office or our workplace somewhere that others feel free to come sit down and even more importantly, let down—a place where they sense belonging. This can be our lives wherever we go. We can carry an atmosphere of belonging that sets people free to just "be."

How can *you* create an atmosphere of belonging in and through your life? These are the family "homes" that so many in the world, especially youth, are crying out for. These are the "family structures" we must start building much more often through all parts of life and society.

The Father's Blessing

I want to share with you a family type exercise of this kind of unconditional love and belonging that is very personal to my family and I (though it is not by any means limited to family in name/blood), one that we have shared and passed on to many more—young and old—all over the world.

When I turned 16, my parents asked if they could give me what they called a "Father's Blessing." It is not referred to as this for gender specificity, or because it has to come from a biological father. Rather, it is called a "Father's Blessing" because we are all created with an innate desire, or need even, to be valued, to be loved, to have purpose and believed be in from a "Father like" position or foundation in our life. Many of us have had the opposite of this given to us, with many fathers out of the picture, and still others who have never received this themselves so they do not know how to pass it on to those around them.

I bring this up for one particular reason: There is a special statement my father spoke over me in this blessing that I have since gone back to often. At that time I didn't realize what a revolutionary statement this was, but I later discovered the power these words held in my life. They are words that set me free to see and live in a renewed way. They are words that were meant for me, that I believe can have great significance for us all:

"I'm very proud to have you carry the LeTourneau name to future generations. I hope you don't believe that I think you're a lesser person because you're not like me in every area of life. That's a common belief among sons of type-A dads. The truth is that I think the best hope for the LeTourneau name lies in the very ways that you're different from me."

My father then went on to highlight and appreciate my differences, not as negative or needing correction, but to appreciate those differences—recognizing these differences not as divisive but as special components that could actually bring more value, hope and life to our family and the world if and when embraced correctly. He didn't just highlight external or behavioral differences, but he highlighted and gave approval to the "special marks of DNA" and the "hidden gold" that he and my mom saw in my identity. This was important for me because I was just coming out of a time in life of really searching for identity, having lost some of my vision for who I was created to be. The blessing, these specific words and what they really meant went on to help me re-discover where my gold had been the whole time, and reminded me to live from that place rather than search or strive for it in other ways or through false versions of identity.

What if we learned to bless and appreciate the differences in others in this way?

What if we recognized that the very best hope for hope itself could be found in many of our differences? And by differences, I'm not focusing on opinions, supporting forms of rebellion, or talking about external differences we often pursue while trying to find our identity. I'm speaking of the unique "Identity-like" DNA kind of differences that we all carry—the kind that we can even become insecure about because we fear that we are less than. Can you imagine a world where our differences didn't divide us, but united us instead? A world where I'm so content with the value *in* me that I can support and bless the value in you? We can stop searching for what has already been freely given to us.

What if we didn't envy one another's gold, but empowered it instead!

Impact of the Father's Blessing

When we arrived in Ethiopia we didn't know where to begin. However, it wasn't long before we started spending time at that local children's home I've already shared a great deal about. As I've said already, this was not your average orphanage. It was a house of hope; they just didn't know it yet. Here is how we helped begin the process of them knowing..

As we spent time with the kids and got to see those treasures up close, we were privileged to see the hope building up from within. They had as much to give the world as we did, we just had to find a way to bring it to the surface and help them see in themselves what—and whom—we saw. I shared about the impact they began to have arising from their difficult circumstances, but what I hadn't shared yet is what helped trigger that vision and belonging that we gave them.

Much of the transformation and empowerment we saw come to life began when we gave them each a "Father's Blessing."

We spent a few more weeks getting to know the kids, taking notes of characteristics and intangibles that marked their lives. We looked for their "gold" so we could highlight it for them to discover with us. We arranged a special ceremony (simply a favorite meal together, but with intention) letting them know we had a surprise for them. We had prepared (and translated) a Father's Blessing for them each, headlined by their name and a photo, and framed for safekeeping.

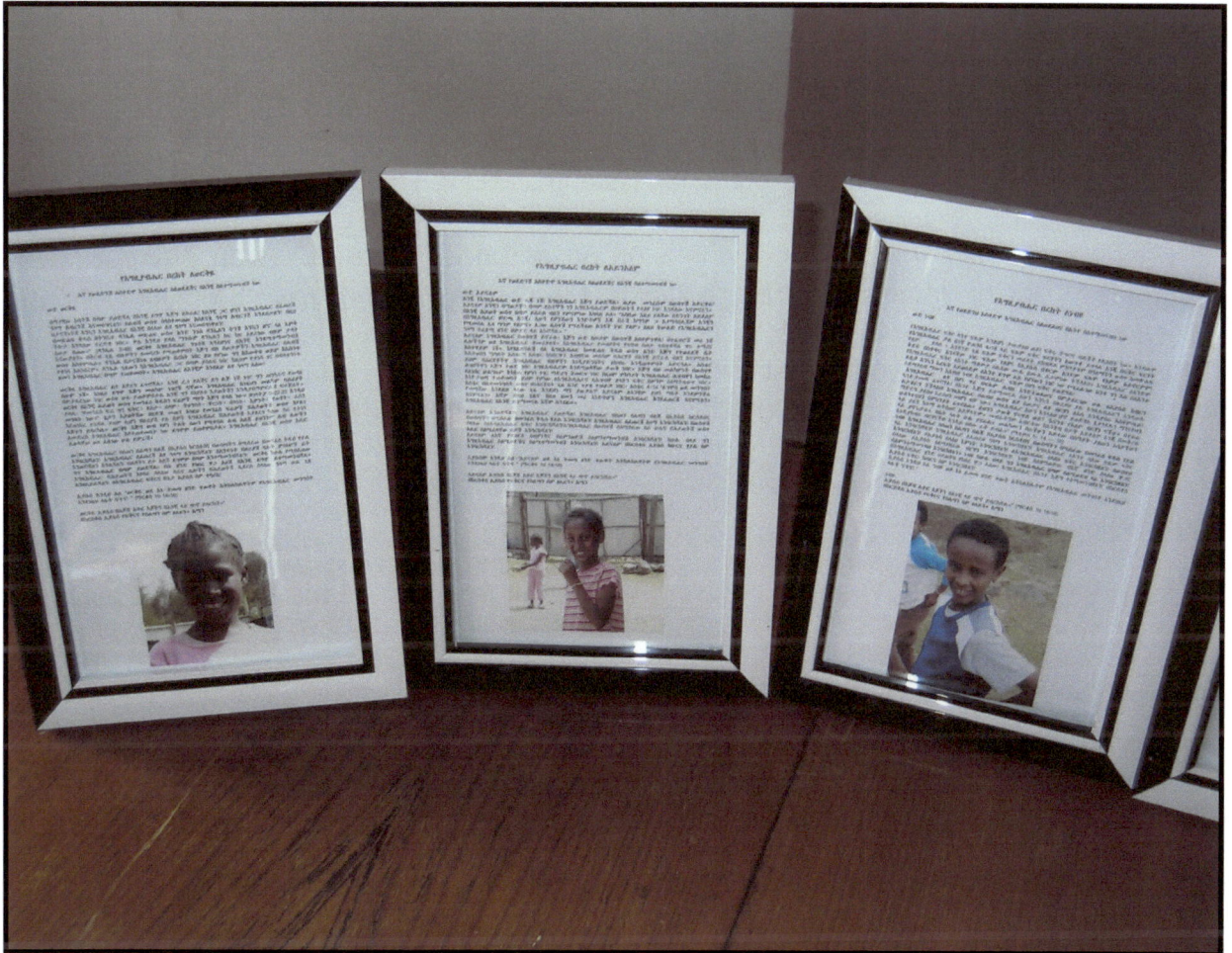

We decided we would begin with the oldest boy, whom we had been told by the facilitators of the home was going through a rough time and hadn't really been himself.

We called him up to us in front of the other kids sitting nearby and we began to read this "Father's Blessing" over him. *I will never forget that moment! It was like watching the sunrise on his life from the bottom of his feet to the top of his head. His whole countenance changed.*

We don't always see something immediate, but with him, it was just what his heart was longing for and from that moment on he became a leader of hope in their group, and home.

The rest of that evening as we gave the Father's Blessing this young man was helping lead the way speaking hopeful encouragements into each of their lives. Not only was he encouraged, he was already living into his potential and making sure others could as well.

It wasn't long after this that the whole group of once "orphans" (who have all been adopted by loving families since) started to help us write and give a similar "Father's Blessing" to the kids we were working with throughout the streets of Addis Ababa, Ethiopia. It was their words that filled the new translated blessing we folded up like a brochure and presented to street children in restaurants during mini banquets. It was those 8 children from that treasure-filled orphanage who became the multipliers of hope, casting it brightly for other kids even less fortunate than them to help them see, receive, and hopefully live.

So, when you look into this section of the Father's Blessing, look at it through this lens of possibility.

You have an opportunity to father/mother hope in their lives.

This is an opportunity to affirm their value, help them dig up their gold, and give them courage to live out their true worth towards the world all around them. Those kids in Ethiopia were the picture for us of what is possible when hope arises in even the most unlikely of places.

Creating a Father's Blessing

There are 4 sections of our *"Father's Blessing"* that we will break down for you section by section before we offer you a sample. These sections are based on our Core Values that everyone, especially youth, long to hear and know:

1. You are VALUED:

- *This is our opportunity as a "father" or "mother" in their life, someone the recipient looks up to, to speak to and affirm the true form of value that we are teaching them about.*

- *When we use words in this format, it doesn't just tell them they have value, but it is actually a way of showing them that value through an intentional act of approval and empowerment.*

- *When you look at the recipient or group—beyond the surface—what attributes of value do they possess?*

- *What intangibles do they carry when they walk into a room?*

- *How does their life encourage yours or others simply by them being who they are?*

- *What do they have to give the world?*

- *If there are negative perspectives they battle with about themselves, speak value to the opposite version of those lies. For example, if they battle self-confidence, than this is a great opportunity to speak to the courage you see in them. Call that courage forward!*

- *Paint a picture through your words of who they truly are from the inside out.*

- *Highlight their gold for them to see!*

2. You are LOVED:

- The most important part of this section is to both say and demonstrate the word "unconditional."

- *Unconditional is a term that needs to become a foundational perspective of their definition of love, and yours!*

- *Unconditional is part of changing their value system by which they measure themselves and others. Such a change can affect their whole life.*

- *Most are raised by a love full of and covered by conditions, how can you help break that off so they can live freely as the one they were created to be?*

- *Unconditional is a form of support regardless of performance.*

- *Unconditional is a form of faithfulness regardless of circumstance.*

- *Unconditional pledges patience with them during their process.*

- *Unconditional expects of ourselves without expecting of them.*

- *Unconditional gives freely and generously in word, love and action.*

- *Are there any specifics you can highlight to tell them "Why" they are loved that DO NOT include "performance"?*

- Unconditional is simply being there for them, standing in their corner, and them knowing you always will be.

- *Some try and be "too cool" to outwardly show they need love and will push it away with a hard or rough edge. Usually, they are the one's wanting it most. They are often waiting for you to give up on them, to reject them or to prove all those past lies as true. But your unconditional love is what will break through that false protection and show them that love is greater than the lie they have been believing.*

- *Speaking and demonstrating love does not have to be a "mushy" or "sappy" thing. There is a genuine, intentional way to impart love like a Mother or Father might, and that is the tone to speak from—a resolutely loving Mother/Father.*

3. You have PURPOSE:

- *Your recipient has a unique and special purpose in this world that no one else has.*

- *Someone, somewhere in the world is waiting for the purpose that your recipient carries.*

- Your words here are to encourage them in hopes that they will see, and live out every bit of purpose they were created for.

- *Be their biggest encourager!*

- *Recognizing they have purpose strengthens their hope.*

- *The world has its own "ready-made" purposes it wants to recruit them for, so we want to bless them forward into the greater purposes they carry to change the world with.*

- *Give them permission to dream into their unique purpose.*

- *Many hide their purpose because it is different from those around them. Help affirm that the uniqueness or "difference" of their purpose is what will make a difference in the world.*

- *If you have seen different or special "hints" of their purpose inside them, speak those out. Encourage them in specifics you've seen in their lives.*

- *Have you seen them make an impact? How?*

- How could you see them helping others through the story they have lived through?

- *What are unique traits and attributes about them that could be part of their purpose?*

- *How can you help give them courage to step forward in their purpose?*

- *Simply put, you are making sure they know that they are important, and have something to give that is valuable.*

4. We BELIEVE in You:

- *We have found this to be one of the most underrated, yet important sections.*

- *It's simple, so be sure not to let familiarity rob what could be given or imparted to them.*

- Everyone wants to be believed in!

- *How many know that they are believed in?*

- *How many can name someone that they know fervently believes in them?*

- *How did it make you feel when you had someone behind you, fully believing in you?*

- *You probably still feel empowered when you have a family member, a boss, a friend or someone else believe in you.*

- *What if they had that too?*

- *What if you gave them that belief?*

- *How far could they go?*

- *How much fuel might you give to their purpose?*

- *How much discouragement might you help eliminate?*

- *Before you write this section to them, really take the time to remember and feel what it was/is like to be believed in so you truly put your heart into it and pass that fuel on to them as well.*

- By believing in them, you are imparting to them vision and courage that their dream, their hope, their purpose, is possible!

- *Use this section to show them the life they were created for.*

A Sample "Father's Blessing"

Dear Participant,

You are VALUED

As the father of six children, I am going to speak to you like I would my own kids, from a father's perspective. There will never be another you in this world— please remember that. You are truly special! No one can measure up to you, and you shouldn't ever try to measure up to someone else either. I am so proud of you, simply for who you are! You bring light, life and joy to the people around you naturally. To look inside you is to see someone so valuable that no price could possibly pay for what you're worth.

However, I cannot value you without also asking you to value yourself in the same. You have to see yourself as more valuable than gold, not in a selfish or proud way, but with confidence and hope. You are not someone who needs to look for worth, for your life and purpose carry the value and worth this world needs most. The seed of that great worth is already inside you just waiting to be watered and given light because your life is full of unending possibility!

You are LOVED

In our world, the meaning of the word love has been stretched out and made far too thin. The world puts pictures in front of us that make us feel like we need to find love or chase it. But what if love is something that we already have? What if you are already loved far more than you know? Many people think that if they can just be noticed, they can perform and that they will finally be loved. We try and build all kinds of stages to lift ourselves up with in hopes that someone will notice and show us some love. But, what if love is the stage you are supposed to shine and live from?

If there is anything I can assure you of, it's that you are loved! I know it might not always feel that way. People are imperfect and don't always know how to show the love they have for you, but that doesn't mean it isn't there. You don't need to search for what you already have. You are loved.

You have PURPOSE

You have gifts in your life that no one else has. You are specially equipped to shine light and give hope to the world in a way that no one else is. You will give life to and impact people in the world that no one else will. Do you realize that someone, somewhere in the world is waiting for the unique purpose that is hidden in you? You were created for a hope and a future, not just for yourself, but a hope and a future for others and the world around you too!

There are people in your life who want to help you find your purpose, and succeed in it. Your purpose is such a powerful thing that it might not always come easy, or as fast as you would like, but it is worth waiting for—and worth looking for. Your purpose is different from anyone else's and cannot be compared to the people around you. One of our greatest hopes in this world is that not one bit of purpose you have been created for will fall to the ground unused. And we want to help you start to live that way. Why? Because...

We BELIEVE in You

Truly, we are writing and sharing this because we believe in you! In fact, I would bet there are more people who believe in you than you even know; they just don't always know how to express it. So we want to take this opportunity to make sure you know how much you are believed in.

You carry something so special that this world needs. You have the ability to reach people that others cannot. You are called to go places that others won't go. We want to be in your corner cheering you on because everyone wants to be part of something—or someone—that they believe in! We want to see people and places changed for the better because of your life. You have something to give that the world desperately needs and we bless you to live out every purpose you have been created for! May your life always be marked with belief!

Now, It's Your Turn!

This is where our love for them, shown and spoken out, begins to give them new eyes to see. Our love, seeing them through the eyes of love, is a huge part of what gives them vision. *Why? How?* It sets them free from insecurity, from false forms of value, free from comparing or striving to measure up to those comparisons. It sets them free to see themselves, the world and others through a new vision. And this is what helps give them a new foundation of love to live *FROM*, instead of live *for*.

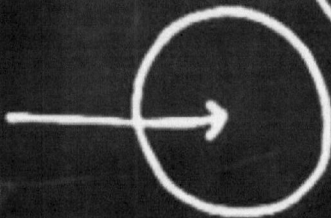

Section Six:
You Have Purpose

I've always contended that you multiply or reproduce who you are much more naturally than you reproduce what you do. Even when a child has a natural talent of what they do passed on to them from a parent, that "doing" comes out of the "who you are" DNA that they received from their parents. It is written like code within us all. So as we look to discover our purpose, we will look within to unearth that other 80% of gifts, talents, hopes and dreams that have perhaps always been inside you, and we'll look to connect the dots of your purpose to help you see, and step forward into such if you haven't already.

We've found that one of the surest ways to cement the value that is in someone, the true, gold-like value that they can live from, is to help them realize that they have something to give. It's a basic foundation of our self-worth.

No matter what your circumstances, or what you do or do not have in your hands, everyone has something to give!

Knowing this can change our whole outlook and give others hope that the worth being spoken over them is not just kind words, but that our value is real and purposeful.

Gousha

We had a number of different groups of street kids that we worked with or took care of in Ethiopia. Some groups were as small as five or six, and some were as big as forty. Though much of our focus was on empowering these kids through identity and purpose, one of the major common denominators among all the kids was their lack of access to food on a consistent basis.

On any given day one or more of the kids may not have eaten over the past twenty-four hours, or more.

Because of their hunger, we tried to at least have snacks available most of the times when we met. And about once a week we'd take each group out to a café for lunch or dinner. If you've eaten Ethiopian food, you'll know that the food typically comes out on a large, shared platter that sits in the middle of the table. The platter is covered in their local staple, injera, which is a thin, spongy, rolled out kind of bread. Then, the injera is covered in whatever meats, veggies, lentils or sauces that you ordered.

Utensils are rarely if ever used while eating Ethiopian cuisine so washing your hands pre-meal is of the utmost importance. This is true for anyone, let alone kids from the streets whose hands are usually cut up, dirty and have been used as tissues. To eat, you simply tear off a piece of the injera and use it to pinch a bite of one of the wonderful delicacies on the platter, then put it in your mouth and enjoy.

This was all new to us when we started traveling to Ethiopia but it's something we fell in love with about the culture once we moved there. However, there was one other cultural twist to eating this way that we were surprised by; something the locals call "gousha."

This custom of "gousha" is when you go through the same process to eat; using the injera to pinch a delicious bite of food but then instead of feeding yourself you reach across the table towards a friend or family member and feed them instead. I have to admit, the first time I experienced someone—without warning—putting a big bite of food in my mouth I was fairly uncomfortable. It wasn't something we experienced too often, but the more we took the street kids to cafés the frequency of such culinary surprises seemed to increase.

And truly, that is one of the places I learned the most.

> See, we were sitting around tables with some of who poverty would say are among the most hungry and food-needy in the world. Some of them hadn't eaten a meal in over a day, let alone had the privilege of enjoying a nice café. Yet, it wasn't when they filled their own empty bellies with food that they were most thankful or joyous, rather, the kids found the most joy when we allowed them to pick up a big bite of food, reach toward our mouths and *feed us*, gousha style.

These most impoverished kids found more hope in giving to us than receiving into their most obvious need!

This is confounding to the very concept of hunger, poverty, and how we usually treat such. Some of the hungriest, most needy kids in the world found more satisfaction in giving something to someone who loved them, whom they loved too.

What this should show us, and what it teaches us about empowerment is that even the most starving people in the world are perhaps *more* hungry for purpose and worth than they are even for food.

When we remember this it sets the table to see how vital it is to give purpose to the next generation, because deep down, no matter what we have or do not have, we all want to be givers in life and not just recipients. We can't tell someone they have worth and value if we're not going prove it by allowing them the opportunity to realize that they too have something to give the world.

Dream

"Imagination is more important than knowledge. For while knowledge defines all we currently know and understand, imagination points to all we might yet discover and create."
– Albert Einstein

To dream is to give life to the identity and the too often "secret hope" that lives within us, a process that can give wings to our soul. We have to let our imagination—and more importantly, our hope—live this freely whether we succeed at first or not. Even the mere process of "dreaming" helps prove that, indeed, we really do have value and purpose.

Dreaming is an exercise of our hope. And hope is one of the foremost staples of life, like the marrow of our bones. Hope is always one of the most powerful things on earth. It is a living force from within us that can flip our attitude, renew our circumstances, or even change the world.

Our personal relationship with hope will always depend on whether we are hope-*sick*, or hope-*full*. If our hope has been delayed, deferred, or even stolen, chances are that our heart has grown cold to all or some of hope's possibilities. This has happened to many, and is truly one of the biggest reasons *The Culture Purple* was birthed. Because no matter where you come from, regardless of what you've been through or see going on around you; hope is still right there to be grasped, and lived.

You already hold the answer deep inside you to seeing your desire for hope fulfilled. And when you do, it will become the tree of life that's been rooted in your heart all along—springing up to grow incredible fruit and turn what *was* your season of famine into a full-hearted feast.

This is where dreaming comes in.

To dream is to imagine hope, it's the freedom and ability to imagine a possibility before it is tangible, or sometimes even before it is rational.

Not all dreams come true, and that's okay, but they do start the road forward, sometimes just to different or even greater dreams.

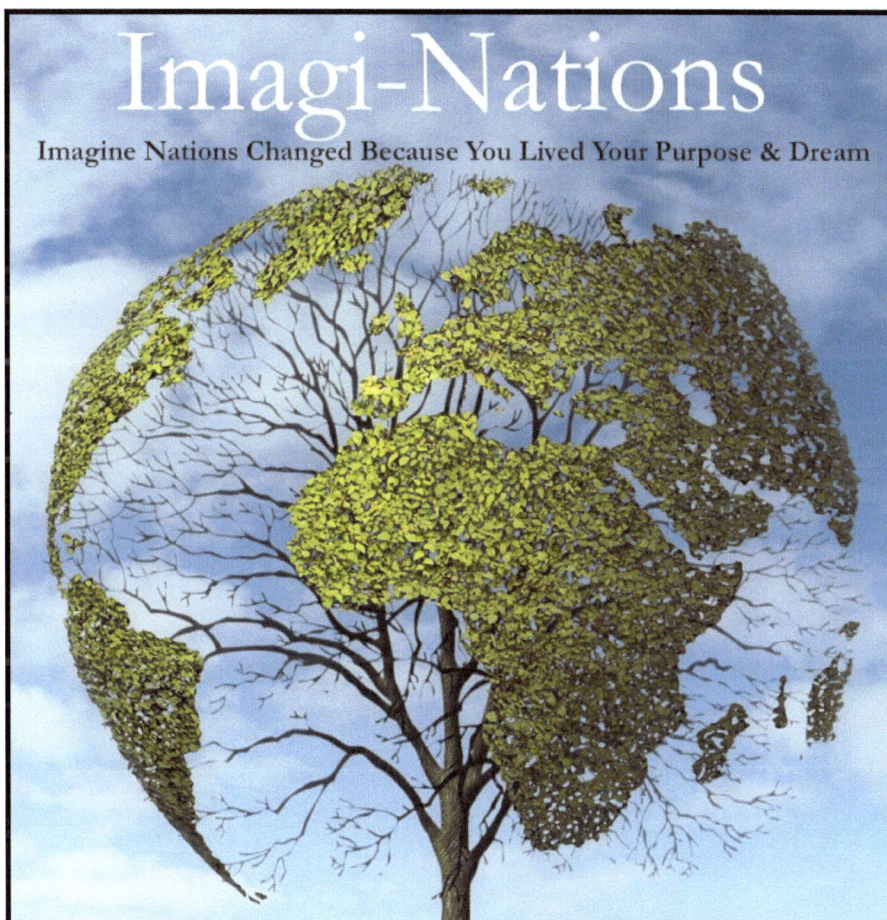

Imagi-Nations

Imagine Nations Changed Because You Lived Your Purpose & Dream

Finding the Hope in Our Dreams

"Hope is the thing with feathers, that perches in the soul. And sings the tune without words, and never stops at all."
                                                    - Emily Dickinson

What is hope?

- *Hope is having a confident expectation of good.*

- *Hope is a yearning for future change.*

- *Hope is seeing something that cannot yet be seen.*

- *What else is hope?*

- *What is hope to you personally?*

What might hope look like for you personally?

- *Does it involve a specific change?*

- *Does it involve a dream or desire?*

What might hope look like for your family?

- *Often, your hope is closely tied to those you love.*

- *How does your hope impact them?*

- *What might it look like if they had hope too?*

What could hope look like in your community, culture, or nation?

-How can/does your personal hope translate to a bigger picture?

-True, lasting hope is not selfish, so how can your hope become hope for someone else?

-Does it bring needed change to or encourage the lives of others?

-Why does your hope help them?

What changes need to happen to see that hope become the new reality? Can you see possible solutions to each necessary change?

- What obstacles are in the way of your hope becoming reality?

- What might be the first changes that need to happen to get started?

- What do you need to learn, understand, or grow in to support your hope becoming a reality?

Is this hope possible? Why? Why not? In most cases, you determine its possibility with how/what you believe.

- Can your hope become more than a dream?

- Yes or no, why do you believe that?

- If "no", why not? What will it take for your "no" to become a "yes"?

- Are there any beliefs you need to change in order to believe your hope can become a reality?

Do you want this hope enough to cross over your doubts and through your circumstances, to believe and persevere until it is realized?

- *Why?*

- *Which parts cause you the most doubt?*

- *Which parts encourage you the most?*

- *Is hope worth it?*

- *Which circumstances look like the biggest opposition to your hope becoming a reality?*

- *How can your hope swallow up or change those circumstances?*

Imagine that light filled picture of hope coming true. It is sitting next to the obstacles that stand in the way. If you are staring at both and have a choice, which picture are you going to feed? Use your vision & belief to make hope bigger.

-*You get to choose which one becomes bigger in your heart and mind.*

-*It's not a one-time choice either, feeding your hope instead of your challenges is an every day, every thought kind of choice.*

-*The world might keep trying to highlight challenges, so you are the one who needs to keep highlighting hope.*

Your belief gives foundation to your hope. I've heard it said that: "faith/belief doesn't deny reality, it defies it." What does this mean? How can you live that statement?

-*Is hope pretending that there aren't challenges? No.*

-*Does faith/belief in your vision of hope mean it will always feel easy? No.*

-Believing in your vision of hope enough to "defy reality" means that you have chosen to feed your hope, instead of your hope being fed to your circumstances.

-As you feed your hope, you nourish something that grows bigger and stronger until it is real enough to devour, or change, your circumstances.

-For example: Imagine you have a lion (your hope) and a wolf (your circumstances). The wolf is there, but if you starve it, the wolf will grow weaker by the day and start to lose its strength. Meanwhile, if you also feed the lion, it will help you overcome the wolf even sooner.

Start Building a Bridge towards HOPE

How do you build a bridge towards hope? By dreaming—and therefore seeing in your heart what hope might look like. This is having "Vision."

- You've already started to develop your vision by imagining what hope might look like. You've given yourself a picture of what is waiting on the other side. Hope is your anchor for the bridge on the other side.

- To take a new step forward in life, you've got to step out to a viewpoint you haven't gone to before. That is the "Ridge of Hope."

- It's a step closer to the edge, away from the comforts of old, comforts that seem nice, but they are often old patterns or old ways of thinking that have little hope, and often hold us in our current circumstances—until we step past them.

- This ridge can be a scary place to stand at first. We're on the edge, staring at a view we've never seen of both the great possibilities and the apparent risk beneath the ridge. But only on the ridge can we begin to position ourselves to build our bridge across. Bridges always start near the edge of something and lead towards our future destination.

- Are you willing to surrender comfort for greater hope and purpose?

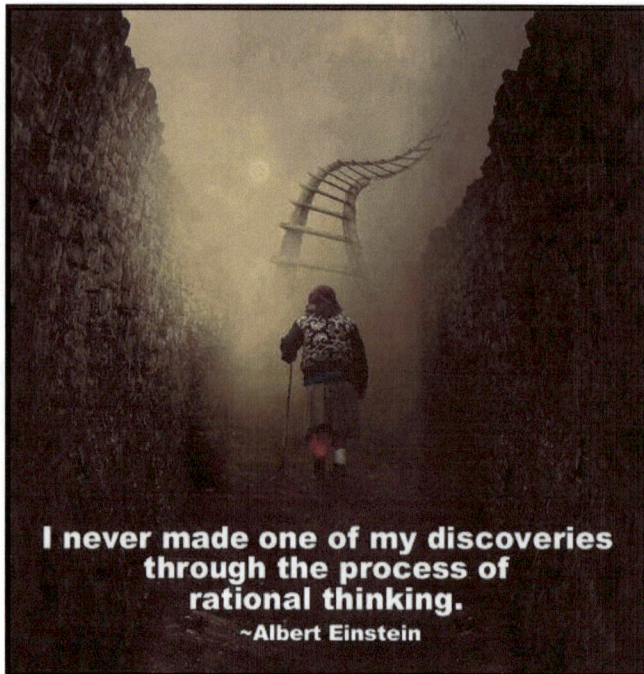

I never made one of my discoveries through the process of rational thinking.
~Albert Einstein

Vision is to see what others do not see, and what you haven't seen previously. It's been said, "change a person's perspective and you can change their whole life." What does this mean?

- Imagine a cliff that overlooks a whole city? You couldn't see all it has to offer until you stepped out a little further, closer to the edge. That's what vision does; it lets you see more so you can find where hope is waiting.

- To discover your vision, your perspective must become like a tall mountain peak that is much higher than your circumstances so that you can see opportunities and possibilities you couldn't see before. Simply put, you must rise higher than your circumstances.

- When you step up to the ridge, you start to confront your fears of not having a purposeful or hopeful future. You tell your insecurities that they won't hold you back any longer.

- So, when you confront your fears by starting to hope and believe for a better future, your fears start to fade further away and you can see what you wouldn't allow yourself to see before.

- Fear tries to hold you in one place, in your comfort zone, and is the opposite of building a bridge. But vision helps you see past your fears, and how to walk forward.

- The hope you are developing helps you recognize the truth that your purpose is bigger than your fears.

The next part of our bridge, after we start to see the hope beyond our fears, is we can use our vision to see and recognize the special purpose that is already inside us, but often hidden from plain sight.

- Like a caterpillar learning to see/believe its wings before it becomes a butterfly.

- The caterpillar may not be able to fly YET, but it starts to recognize the great possibility of wings it has inside so it can begin to look forward and prepare.

- You weren't just created to have hope; you were created to be a big part of that hope.

- You have hope inside you. You have wings inside you. A caterpillar may move slowly and feel small and insignificant much of its life, but its own unique wings have always been hidden inside waiting to be recognized.

- Do you believe you have that kind of hope inside? Why?

Belief for purpose must be part of the foundation for our bridge, even if we do not fully know what that purpose is yet.

- Knowing we have purpose is a big part of our "Why." It helps motivate us that this new and sometimes challenging journey towards hope is worth it, and believing we have purpose helps remind us that we are worth it, that we carry value that the world needs.

- How do you feel when you know you have value?

- Do you want to add value to the world and bring hopeful impact to others?

- Do you believe you can, and will?

- We will spend plenty of time discovering "what" your purpose is. For now, believing you have one helps remind you "why" you are moving forward—especially for when it's hard.

Knowing we have a purpose is vital, because the ridge of Hope is where we are confronted with a decision.

- Will we step forward towards this new, possible reality of greater hope?

- We make a decision of how we will think, what we will expect, and why we will persevere.

- Purpose helps strengthen those decisions.

- Will we stay where we are at in order to guarantee survival? Or...

- Will we "risk" our fears and leave them behind?

- Will we decide that we don't just want to see hope, but actually live it?

Fear is a bully from a false reality that tries to intimidate us—until we confront those fears by stepping past them.

- Fear is the biggest liar, don't listen to it.

- Fear's perspective comes from trying to see the future through negative circumstances that worry about what might happen.

- *Overcoming Fear's Perspective – Fear is nothing more than a vision of a false reality that seeks to be supported by current circumstance, and proven true by lack of new action. You can prove fear wrong!*

- *Don't negotiate with your fears; they are only trying to steal hope from your future.*

- *Fear might keep trying to pop up each step of the way, but with every thought you think, you have the choice of whether you will believe your fears, or if you believe your hope.*

We take these steps internally with our thoughts first.

- *Are you using your vision to imagine your fears?*

- *Or are you using your vision to build a bridge towards hope?*

- *What you visualize and believe on the inside is what you will build on the outside.*

You determine your bridge, so what kind of bridge will you build?

- *Keep your internal eyes—your vision—on hope and this will make every plank of wood in your bridge stronger for you to keep stepping forward on.*

- *Hope's perspective rises higher above the challenges of the day so that it can see the possibilities of "how" we can overcome each step of the way.*

- *Believe in your vision, believe in yourself and believe that the hope you want is possible. Why is your belief important? It is what feeds your hope.*

- *Remember, you were created with value and purpose, even if you don't see it yet. See it with your belief! You carry a big portion of the hope you want to see. Your purpose needs to get to the other side because the world is waiting for what is inside of you.*

Imagine the Way Forward

"To IMAGINE is not merely to daydream; to imagine is our first opportunity to see and give life to a hopeful future."

We must continue to harness and use our imagination for each STEP of the way.

- *Most often think that using our imagination is to have our head in the clouds without ever doing anything. This doesn't have to be the case. We can use our imagination for SO much more!*

- *We can use our imagination as a preview of our steps, seeing them before we take them. Visualizing somewhere before we actually get there.*

- *Our imagination can also help prepare or "pave" the way for our steps forward by preparing our thoughts and expectations for the journey and how to overcome along the way.*

Imagine good and positive "what if's" instead of negative "what if's".

- *For example: When we worry about something, we are often imagining negative "what if" scenarios we are afraid of happening. When we worry in this way, it's the opposite of preparing the way. Instead, this worry is almost like putting obstacles in our way to climb over.*

- *So, if we are already using our imagination so powerfully, why not use it for the positive?*

- *How can you imagine positive "what if's" instead of negative one's? How will that help you?*

- *It can help you recognize opportunities you might have otherwise missed.*

- To imagine the positive "what if's" is a way to learn to "dream big" or to start dreaming about what might be possible that isn't yet.

- For example: If you are going on a trip, don't spend your time imagining the negatives that could happen. Be prepared, but, imagine the good kind of surprises that could happen too. Who might you meet? What opportunity might you run into?

It is a battle of the mind that we must win every step of the way. Every thought that we have must be taken captive and not allowed into our beliefs until we are certain it is a true, hopeful and loving thought.

- It's very easy to fall back into this kind of negative worry, so we must stay on guard in our mind. If we guard our mind from these things, then the negatives have less possibility of getting into our actual lives.

- Don't just believe anything that you worry about. Worry is a breeding ground for lies.

- What are some areas you tend to worry about more than others?

- How can you flip those to think of them, or imagine them in an opposite, hopeful way?

Becoming an optimist isn't enough to overcome pessimists or realists, instead we must think like an opportunist. What does this mean? An "Opportunist" sees possibility when the world says there is none AND finds a way to grab hold of even the slightest opportunity.

- What is an optimist? This is someone who always sees the positive in something.

- What is a realist? This is someone who sees things just as they are, not as negative, but they don't usually see the hidden hope either.

- What is a pessimist? This is someone who always sees the negative in something.

- What is an opportunist? This is someone who always sees an opportunity in something, instead of just seeing it as it is.

- Which one is most powerful? Why?

- How could being an "opportunist" affect your ability to move forward into hope? You would see the chance to make something better.

- An opportunist is solution oriented. No matter what happens, they are not just looking for the positive, they are finding ways to create the positive.

We must learn to use our imagination for the creation of good, first inside our mind, with the full support of our heart, then decide to turn what was imagination into an act of our will.

- If you imagine something as possible, you are more likely to believe it as possible.

- If you believe something might be possible, you are more likely to invest your heart into stepping out and trying.

- If you start to try, you are more likely to persevere until your hope is realized.

- What is something you have always wanted to do but thought you couldn't?

- Imagine it being possible. Now, start to invest your heart into it by imagining what you would feel if it actually happened. You're probably imagining something that brings you joy! Does that feeling of joy make you want to start pursuing it to make it possible in reality?

When we learn to Imagine HOPE, we will create a VISION in our heart and mind that gives us the WILL to keep stepping FORWARD until that hope is realized by us, and others.

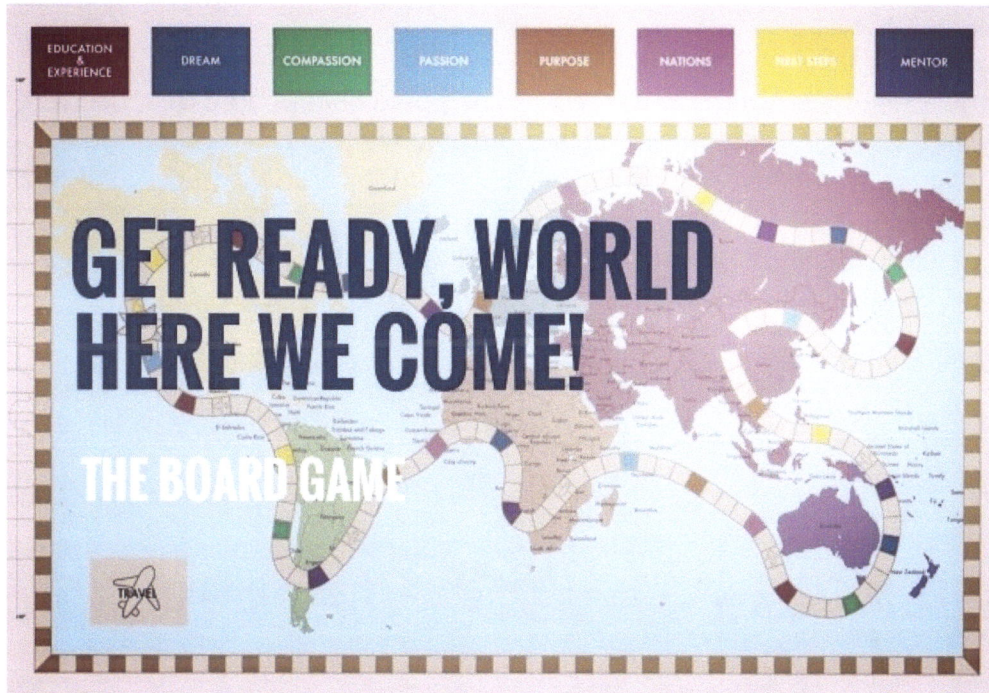

Your Dream

Let's start to discover and plan our dream in a more personal and practical way.

We have developed a process that helps us discover and live out our unique purpose. **This process of purpose starts with dreaming and will continue through subjects like: Compassion, Passion, Purpose (or Method), Nations, and First Steps.** But first, let's start by planning our "Dream."

What do you want to give the world?

If you could give *anything*, to *anyone*, *anywhere*—in a very broad sense—what would it be? Here are a few general ideas to help get you started as we want to choose a broad dream of what you want to give first, and then it will get narrowed down and sharpened through the other categories of the process later.

- Do you want to give them LOVE?
- Maybe you want to bring PEACE.
- Or how about JOY?
- What if you gave people COURAGE?
- Many people need SECOND CHANCES! - You could give people EDUCATION.
- What about FAMILY? There are many people who want to feel like part of a family.
- Maybe you have an inventor's mind. You could give the world NEW IDEAS AND INVENTIONS.
- And as we know many people need all kinds of different RESOURCES.
- Maybe you could give people JOBS or other OPPORTUNITIES?

What do you dream of giving the world?

Why?

How could giving such change the lives of others?

In what ways have others given you the very thing you dream of giving the world?

What other personal experiences have you had with the subject you dream of giving to the world?

What did it feel like when you experience your own need for this, or when you saw the need in others?

Do you know anyone around you, perhaps in your family, school or community who is good at giving to others in this way? Who? If not, start asking those you trust about someone who has experience in this way.

Have you considered asking them to talk about your dream so you can learn from them?

What questions would you like to ask them?

How can you start to practice your dream or begin giving it to others in smaller ways? For example: If your dream is "to give Courage to the world" perhaps you could practice every day by saying something really positive and hopeful to three people each day to give them a boost. That would be a good short-term goal to get started.

The Power of "Compassion"

"The purpose of life is not to be happy. It is to be useful, to be honorable, to be compassionate, to have it make some difference that you have lived and lived well."
- Ralph Waldo Emerson

After we dive into dreaming about what we want to give to the world, our next step is to recognize our area of compassion. Now, we all probably have multiple areas that move our hearts with compassion. But in this section we are going to try and help identify one primary, powerful engine that drives your "why" and actually multiplies your impact.

Compassion is one of the most powerful dynamics in the world. It is not self-based nor agenda driven. It acts as an engine or the heartbeat behind our purpose and dream because it is an inward desire or fiery burn within you that wants to help bring an answer to a particular kind of hurt or need.

It is a selfless form of desire that fights for another with love, *and from love*. Compassion gives beyond the mind's capacity and lends power that is hidden in our hearts and *from* our personal experience. Before we go further in learning to identify and use our compassion, let me show you the power of compassion at work.

Inside-Out Transformation: "Berhanu"

When we lived in Ethiopia and were working with groups of kids on the streets, one fourteen year-old boy came into our family that impacted us all. His name was Berhanu (changed for privacy) and from the outside he was not like most of the other kids we cared for or worked with. Berhanu had lost both of his arms at his shoulders in a train accident when he was eleven.

In one sense, we were amazed by Berhanu; watching all he had learned to do without limbs. He would pick up a pencil with his toes and start writing, or jump on our computer and Google something with his feet. He had learned to adapt. However, he was also hurting greatly.

Like many of the other kids on the streets, Berhanu had come from a down-country rural area. He and his family battled poverty, brokenness and division in the home, and so, as many of the kids do he ran to the city in search of some form of hope. Instead, he found local drugs and a life on the streets without much warmth—inside or out.

In our group times we watched Berhanu and the other kids interact and it would just drop our hearts to the floor. To see them serve him sips of tea, or feed him bread let us see the compassion alive in his peers, peers who also were mostly just surviving in their own battles; and yet here they were serving him. In the same breath, we watched Berhanu time and again having to humble himself to receive even the most basic things from others day after day.

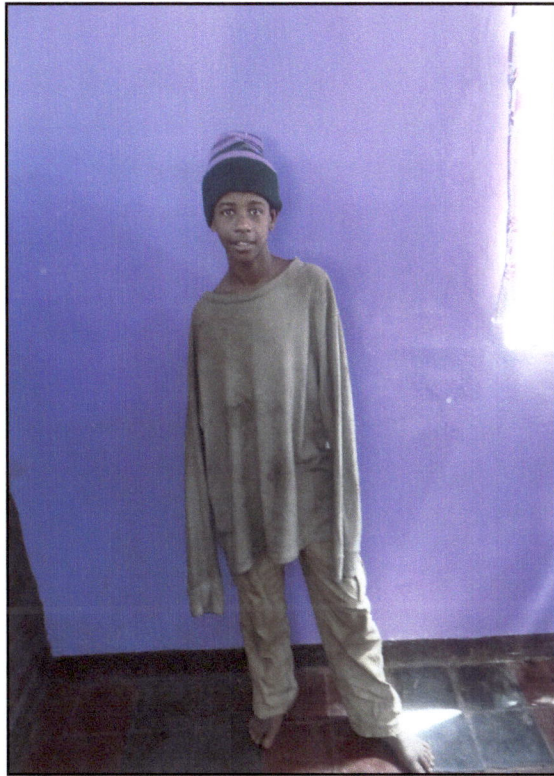

("Berhanu" when he first joined our group.)

Our family and our leadership team desperately wanted change for Berhanu. We sought to help meet basic physical needs as we had the other kids, and also like the others we gave him supplies or tools to help him earn small amounts of money while on the streets; things like shoe-shine boxes or a tray of items the kids would often sell. This helped a lot of the kids, but for Berhanu it only made his needs that much more obvious.

Every time we bought him goods to sell on a tray that he could carry, strapped to him around his neck, he would come back a couple days later empty handed because a stranger had stolen the goods off his neck and reached into his pockets to take all the cash he had earned.

It was heartbreaking to watch and we needed better solutions than these external provisions.

We were in the middle of setting up a shelter to house all of the kids, but it was still weeks away from being finished. However, we knew Berhanu needed more immediate care than the other kids so we invited him to live in our family home until the shelter home was ready. It was then that I tapped a little deeper into the power of compassion.

I realized that I couldn't truly help Berhanu to the extent that we all desired to if I didn't know what he was actually going through. And though I could never understand fully, I felt like I needed a little more of a glimpse into his world to love him better and have greater compassion towards what he really needed for change.

I had an idea: I would pick a busy day in my week and for those twenty-four hours I would go without using *my arms*. I figured I could bandage them tightly to my body and then, just *maybe,* feel even half a percent of what he feels so I could better understand his battle. First I needed to ask permission to do this, from Berhanu and from my wife, Destiny.

For Berhanu, I wanted to make sure he knew that in no way was I mocking him or trying to be funny. I didn't want to have him misunderstand my motives in any way.

I wanted him to know I took this very seriously because I wanted to be able to care for him in a more powerful way.

And from my wife, well, I needed her permission because as you can imagine, without arms, well, I would need a lot of personal "help" that day if you know what I mean.

Both Berhanu and my wife were on board and I decided I would begin at 10pm the night before a busy day that we were planning to be out and about with a lot of our programs. I slept terribly that night, not being able to position my arms the way I wanted to in balancing the position I slept in. Because of this, I had a constant awareness of my lack, even while sleeping. And as you can probably imagine, I needed A LOT of help the next day. I couldn't feed myself, I couldn't drive like normal, I couldn't pick up my kids, I couldn't even go to the bathroom on my own.

It was mentally and physically exhausting—and most of all, it was hope-crushing.

See, I'm a very purposeful person who loves to dream and go after those dreams—and help others do the same. But I couldn't even open my laptop computer by myself. To type one sentence in an e-mail with my nose took forever and was completely draining.

It was so hard to find purpose, and because of that I could feel my hope starting to wane.

On top of that, I had to rely on someone else for everything I did, or wanted to do. To have very little self-sufficiency made my hope swirl down the drain even faster, while taking all my pride with it.

> That's when I realized what Berhanu really needed. I had compassion for him at a deeper level and came to the conclusion that as much as I would like to give him new arms or better outward circumstances, what Berhanu really needed was a restored heart and hope. In one day I felt the crushing blows to my heart of worthlessness, purposelessness and more; how many of these same hits did he take every day? Berhanu didn't just need new arms; he needed a healed heart.

From that point on our family and team took a different approach in restoring Berhanu. We came around him and blessed him at a heart level, trying to refill his tank with hope and purpose. We spoke into his self worth and did what we could to restore his heart.

It was almost overnight that we saw a difference begin in him, and over the next two weeks he took leaps and bounds forward in life, even being reconciled to his own family down country. His cycles and patterns changed because he was seen and restored from the inside, out. And it all began by tapping into the power of compassion.

Identifying Our Compassion

"He who has a 'why' to live for can bear almost any 'how.'"
— Friedrich Nietzche

Our "Why" can be attributed to many forms of internal motivation and vision, but I believe that recognizing and feeding our specifically directed "Compassion" will strengthen our perseverance and exponentially multiply our output. Operating out of—*and in*—a compassion is one of the greatest ways to ensure that our purpose is not just a surface solution, but a stream of impact that flows from our soul and to those same deeper needs in others.

Compassion pulls on our personal experience—what we have been through or watched others go through—to give us greater empathy and more powerful love for someone else who is going through the same thing. Drawing from our personal experience allows us to feel someone's pain and then have deeper cause or reason to help see restoration come to life.

Compassion is that feeling somewhere deep inside where you feel pain or hurt for someone else and what they are going through. We all have moments where we feel more compassion than we do at other times. It is both okay, and important, that your compassion is different than others around you because we each are created and purposed to impact the world in a different way and our compassion is something of a heartfelt compass to help steer that impact.

Some of us feel extra compassion for people who are going through something that we too have gone through. Maybe you've watched a close family member battle a difficult sickness, so when you see someone who is affected by the same illness you feel an extra measure of compassion for them because your heart understands part of what they are going through.

What this also shows us is that the trials we experience, or see around us, are difficulties that can be transformed into something that teaches us how to give life to others!

For instance, if you have grown up in a broken family, you know how that has affected you and what it has taken to overcome those hardships. So, you also know how to help others walk through those difficulties and come out with true light on the other side.

Here are some examples of what may ignite your compassion:

- Broken Families
- Orphans
- Those battling sickness or disease
- Homelessness
- Widows
- Slavery and/or trafficking
- Victims of abuse
- Those impacted by addiction
- Those battling mental illness
- The elderly
- Those who need food or water
- Need for education
- Bullying
- Disunity between race, ethnicity or other
- Hopelessness
- At-risk youth
- …What would you add?

* Have you noticed what injustice is taking place when you find your heart breaking for someone or wanting to help on their behalf? Why?

* What types of movies or scenes make you tear up or cry whenever you see them? Why? You might find a pattern that will help you identify your compassion.

For example, one of my daughters can become extremely emotional when she sees or hears of injustice to babies. So, obviously, one of her compassions is newborn babies and those still in the womb.

What about you?

* What hard or difficult things have you or your family and friends gone through in life? Do these experiences have an impact on your heart and what/who you feel compassion towards?

* Do you see a pattern in any of your answers?

* What do your answers or the patterns within your answers tell you? Who or what is your compassion extra drawn towards?

* How often do you personally use your compassion to reach out to those your heart hurts for? When was the last time you did? What happened?

* Does focusing on your compassion motivate you? How? Why?

* How do you see the injustice that is tied to your compassion lived out around you on an every day basis?

Now that you've identified your compassion it will be easier and more natural to recognize it on a daily basis and see opportunities to life purposefully and give life to others.

Studying Our Compassion

Spend the next several days paying extra attention to those around you affected by your areas of compassion. Watch, observe and grow in your understanding; take notes and journal each day.

* How and why are they negatively affected?

* Are there any patterns in their life or patterns in the culture that are impacting them?

*What do they need?

* Why might they need those things?

* What might be keeping them from receiving or living those answers? Remember, every situation or person might be very different or be caused by different circumstances.

* The goal isn't just to have the answers for them, but to understand where they are coming from so you can relate to them in a greater way. How are you learning to understand your compassion in a greater way?

* Find ways to study your area of compassion. Use the internet, read books, find people to ask questions, or learn directly from people who either are affected by that injustice or who are working to help that area.

Write down 5 things about your area of compassion that you believe are most important to recognize:

1.

2.

3.

4.

5.

* Our compassion is often led by our heart and love, which is very important. But we also watch, study and learn so that we can understand and gain wisdom. How has your perspective grown about your area of compassion? Are you more prepared to love others well? Why? How?

Activating Our Compassion

Now that we've started to allow wisdom and understanding to start to catch up to what we feel in our heart, it's time to allow our heart of compassion to flow out and practice sharing the "Dream" we want to give others from Stage 1, while doing so through the "Compassion" that we are discovering here in Stage 2.

Who/where is someone in your community that struggles with the very injustice that your compassion loves to answer?

* What do you have in your heart, or in your hands, that can help? You may have a talent, you may have resources, or you may simply have time to give. Perhaps it is simply giving them love through words or acts of kindness. What do you have that could be given through your compassion?

Now, think back to your "Dream," this will help you remember what you have in your heart, or in your hands, to give to others. You have more value to give than you realize. So, what do you have?

* How can you start to share it with them? Who might be able to join you and help?

* Use your compassion 3 different times to reach out to those you have identified. It could be volunteering somewhere, or it could be something very simple. But make sure you have permission or someone with you before you begin. Then, write down what you experienced each of the 3 times you put your compassion into action.

Day 1 -

What happened? How did you step out with compassion?

How did they receive your compassion?

What did you learn to help you next time?

Day 2 –

What happened? How did you step out with compassion?

How did they receive your compassion?

What did you learn to help you next time?

Day 3 –

What happened? How did you step out with compassion?

How did they receive your compassion?

What did you learn to help you next time?

When we start to serve others with our compassion, it's important that we do not go from a place of passion to a place of duty. Always remind yourself why you are serving others that way. It's not about our agenda, rather, it's about serving them with our compassion. We need to understand them as we give, not just give out of our own perspective.

Your "Compassion" is your "why" and helps you stay motivated by the passion that ignited your heart in the first place. Your compassion is a fire that you never want to let burn out.

* Because of that, please share again WHY you have the specific compassion that you do? What does your compassion mean to you?

Imagine with us: How will your compassion make a difference in the world?

Your Passion

This subject and stage in our journey is simple, but very important. The primary question we want to ask you is:

What do you love to do? What are you passionate about?

Many people try and decide between three different choices, one of pursuing something they love to do (such as music, art or sports), or towards making money, or choosing to pursue their area of compassion and desire to help others who are hurting. But, we don't necessarily think it has to be a choice of one or the other. We believe that you were created with purpose that can work all three of those things together for you, and others.

When you take your compassion for others in the world and then combine it with your passion and what you love, more often than not you will discover your purpose.

The two areas don't need to be separate. You can use your passion to help serve, love and reach out to those you have compassion for.

You may have a love for music and a desire to succeed in that area; that's a good thing! Your desire in that area is powerful! Many think you have to take a passion like music and either become a star performer, or simply keep it as a hobby. But there are so many other options. Your desire to play music can help many people in many different ways. The same goes for something like sports, art, business, technology, building, cooking, and so much more! You can use these passions as a way to connect with or serve those you have compassion for.

We want to help you recognize your passion in life for the things you love and then look at how your passion can be combined with both your "Dream" and your "Compassion" to impact the world in a life-giving way.

* Here is a list of interests that many people are passionate about, but obviously there are a lot more beyond this list. What is yours?

- Art
- Music
- Sports
- Technology
- Science
- Business
- Healthcare
- Building & Construction
- Food & Hospitality
- Education
- Government
- Entertainment
- Animals
- Books
- Travel
- Creativity & Design
- Math
- Nature
- Other?

* So, what do you love? What are you passionate about? And please explain why. There might be more than one, and that's okay too.

* How would it make you feel for your passion to always be a big part of your life? Why?

* How would it make you feel to not only get to live your passion, but to be successful at it? Why?

* What if the thing you love to do also helped change the lives of people you love? How would that be rewarding for you, and for them?

Imagine

Now, take a few minutes of quiet time by yourself. Close your eyes and start to picture yourself joyfully living out your passion. See yourself learning and growing to a point of great success. Now, imagine your success having a life-giving impact on the world. Imagine that your desire or passion being fulfilled also gave life to others in positive, life-changing ways.

* What did you see yourself doing?

* As you were imagining this, how did you feel?

* What part of it brought you the most joy?

* What part of your passion might bring hope and life to others?

* Now, are you even more hopeful about your passion than before? Why?/How?

* What did you learn about your passion from looking at it in a new, focused way?

* What did you learn about yourself?

Growing In Your Craft

* Now, it's time to invest in what you love. The best thing you can invest into your passion is time. To be successful in our passion, we must give it consistent time and energy on an ongoing basis to help it grow.

* What are 3 ways you can practice your passion?

1.

2.

3.

* How will you implement these ways into your daily life? How can you be consistent in practicing your passion? How often will you practice? How many hours per day? How many days per week?

Remember, always give yourself at least one day per week to rest from the investment you are putting in. Consistent rest combined with hard work will help you be better in the long run.

* In the next spaces begin to write out a plan of when and how you will practice consistently.

Monday:

Tuesday:

Wednesday:

Thursday:

Friday:

Saturday:

Sunday:

* What are some goals you have? Why?

* How will your goals help you, and others?

Putting the Pieces Together

* From Stage 1, what was your "Dream" of what you want to give to the world? Has it changed at all? Has it grown bigger? How?

* From Stage 2, what is your "Compassion"? Is it easier to recognize now? Is your compassion for others growing? Does it make your love grow bigger?

* And now, how can you combine your "Dream" with your "Compassion" to add even more meaning and impact to your PASSION? Think of it this way:

I want to give (DREAM) to (COMPASSION) through (PASSION).

For example: I want to give "courage" to "orphans" through "sports."

Or

I want to give "peace" to "victims of abuse" through "music".

Are you beginning to realize you have more purpose inside you than you thought?

Do you see that you already have amazing worth inside you and something important to give the world around you?

You have been created with special attributes inside of you designed for you to give life, hope and love to others. Now, we you can get creative in how you might live this out.

Imagine

* In 1 year, how might your life be different by focusing on your dream, your compassion, and your passion? Describe what your life might look like then:

* In 5 years, how could the world be different because you started to give life to others through these special parts of your life?

Imagine how much JOY you and others will find as you begin to discover and live the life you were created for.

Living Purpose:

You've taken some incredible steps to get so far towards living out your purpose and dream. You have started a new beginning for your life, and eventually for many others too. You are on a very special and important journey.

You have not only decided to dream but you have decided to step forward and believe that the purpose you have been created for—the purpose already inside of you—can and will be lived out! No matter what anyone says, no matter where you come from or what you have gone through—believe us—you and your life do have great purpose!

> Our hope in this journey with you is that you will see who you were created to be, and how you were created to live that out to make a difference in the world. We don't want to see any part of your purpose fall to the ground. We believe you have something that the world eagerly needs.

Freeze Tag

We opened a boys home for about forty of the street kids in Ethiopia. It was on a good sized property—for there at least—and allowed us to all play some fun games outside together. One time, we decided to teach them the game freeze tag, which they had never heard of let alone played before.

When those of us who know the game play it we typically have certain strategies to protect ourselves from being tagged. You know what happens, you kind of try and linger away from everyone, by yourself, trying to protect yourself from being noticed, or tagged. But when we taught these kids in Ethiopia they saw right through the game. They weren't afraid of being tagged, thus feeling the need to play the game defensively. If I was "it," they'd stay right in a group all around me knowing that even if I tagged them there were five more friends already right there to unfreeze them. This gave them an "offensive" mindset to playing the game.

Instead of playing the game afraid and defending themselves from possibly getting frozen, they played it offensively, daring me to try to be able to get them all at once, knowing I couldn't ever tag that many people that quickly.

It was fascinating to watch the mindset they chose. And it is a picture to how we should all be doing life and empowering others to do life as well.

Offense vs. Defense

Much of western culture in particular can be very "fear based" in nature. Much of life is built around protections of some sort, whether that be insurance and the "what if's" of life or the insecurities and how we strive so much to cover up those areas. In many ways we are trained to be very "defensive" minded. And truly, that's why empowering others doesn't happen as often as it should. We tend to think of all the things that could go wrong. We worry about what will happen if that person messes up and fails, and how that might reflect upon us personally or organizationally. We focus on the negative "what if's" and we position ourselves at all cost to avoid getting frozen, when what we should be doing is focused on the possibilities of playing offense.

If I empower this person, what if it changes their life, or many lives? If I step into my purpose, what if I find significance and value that is bigger than all the insecurities I've been covering for all these years? If I step forward and take this risk, what if I find meaningful purpose?

An offensive mindset is essential to finding our purpose, and even more important to consistently walking in it. Purpose isn't easy, and it rarely comes and knocks on our door without us stepping out, putting ourselves in a place of courage, and putting more value in purpose than we do in protection.

We need to learn to do life and purpose the way the kids in Ethiopia played freeze tag—with freedom, and always looking to take ground.

Discovering Your Purpose

So, in this stage of our journey we want to look together at what you might do to live out your dream. For example, if you are going to travel in a new direction across the country or across the world, you have to decide how you will travel? Will you go by car, by airplane, by train, by helicopter, by truck or by boat? The same "How" applies here. What will be your vehicle to live out your purpose in your family, community, culture and world?

* Here is an example. Let's say that your dream is to give "hope" to "those who are homeless" and you're going to use your passion for "business" to do this. That would be an incredible purpose. So, *how* will you give them hope through business?

Will you start a business? Will you offer teaching and training about business? Will you open a facility where they can come and learn? Will you offer them supplies to help them get started? Or will you use another way? There are many different ways you can live out your purpose towards the world.

So, for your purpose, how will you give your dream to those you have compassion for? Will you:

- Write something to benefit them
- Open a facility
- Speak on their behalf
- Teach or train them
- Mentor or coach them
- Offer supplies or resources that they need
- Start a business to help fund their new beginning
- Travel to encourage them
- Or maybe something else??

* Which purpose is one you would choose?

* Why did you choose this way of applying your purpose? Is it because you have experience in that area? Is that something you've always wanted to do? Do you have special talent in that area of life?

Practical Steps for Your Purpose

* What might you need to accomplish this purpose? What will you need to get started?

* You might not have access to everything you need yet to fulfill the big version of what you dream, but you can still start small. What do you already have that you can use to get started in a small way? Every big dream and impact begins with one small, faith-filled step of hope and love.

* Who do you know that could help you get started? Who are your biggest supporters or encouragers? Why or how might they be able to help? Have you talked to them yet? When can you set up a time to talk with them and share your dream?

* What education or training might you need to get started? Maybe your dream doesn't require specific or formal education, but it still requires learning. What do you need to learn about the "How" of your purpose?

* How can you start to gain experience? Is there somewhere you can volunteer to help? If so, where? Is there something you can start to put your purpose into practice?

* What resources are necessary to get started? Always remember, focus on what you DO HAVE instead of what you don't have. You don't need to have all the answers to begin, just a willingness to take that first step. What do you need to get started in a simple way?

There are often many stages to seeing your purpose and dream lived out.

For example: If you want to open a facility to help the homeless and don't have a place yet, maybe you can start by sharing your dream with friends and family to gather clothes or food to take to the homeless one piece at a time.

Or...

If your dream is to help orphans through music through teaching; maybe you can begin by practicing music with other youth around you who have never played music before.

No matter what your dream is or how you want to change the world, there are always small ways that you can begin. Don't ever feel bad about small beginnings; everyone has to start somewhere.

Every great work has a first step. The important question is, how you will start yours?

Imagine

* Imagine that you are starting to live your purpose and lives are being changed. What will it look like? What might your days look like? What is happening? How are lives being touched through your purpose?

* Is it fun to make a difference in the world? How do you feel? Why? Are you happy? Do you feel this is what you were created to do? Does it bring you JOY? Does it bring joy to others?

*Your imagination will help you see your dream become reality even before it happens. It will keep your passion and joy alive. It will help you imagine all the good "What if's" that could happen.

- What if you really did give hope to the world?

- What if your compassion changed the world for 1 person, or many more?

- What if you really did take that first step?

- What if it happened even better than you could dream?

Never stop picturing your dream with your imagination; it helps you keep moving forward!

Planning

* When will you meet with someone who can support and encourage you in your purpose?

* What will you share with them?

It's important that you can clearly tell them WHY this purpose is important to you, and WHY it is important to the world. When you meet with them, be prepared. Let them see your heart and passion for WHY you want to live this dream.

* When will you start?

Nations

We've come to one of my favorite parts of our journey. This is when we open our eyes and expand our dreams to look across the nations. We must realize that the world is smaller than we think and learn to believe that anything is possible when we know who we were created to be.

We might not all be called to the nations, and we might be called right where we currently are; it is important though to look up and know what's possible, to know how to see beyond our circumstances and step into our value and purpose no matter how near or how far. Believing for nations is another way that we remove unnecessary limits.

So, now it's time to discover WHERE our hearts feel called to bring hope in the world.

When I was growing up I always had a heart for Africa. I loved learning about the cultures, hearing the music, and reading or watching stories of the people groups. Then I met my wife, Destiny, when I was 16, and one of the many things that linked our hearts together was our mutual love for the continent of Africa, as she had a similar dream. That dream continued and eventually I traveled to the nation of Nambia in the southern part of Africa when I was 18 years old. Then, I visited several more nations across Africa with my wife and one of our daughters when I was 26. And then, the next year we moved our family to live in Ethiopia. My heart for Africa became a dream that kept growing bigger, and bigger. It didn't happen right away, but I never let that love fade away, and eventually, my wife and I both saw it all come true. Now, our kids dream in that same manner with their own hope and calling.

When you dream about your purpose, we want you to feel free to dream of nations! Whether you are called to your own country or another nation, it is important to develop a worldwide perspective.

I love looking at maps of the world! When I walk through an office or school with a big map on the wall, I often can't help myself but to look all across the world and study the nations, dreaming about where I would love to visit and the incredible people and cultures in those places. I start to imagine what it would be like to visit each place. And with some of those nations I even add them to my dream list.

Imagine that there is a big map in front of you and you can go anywhere in the world!! *Where would you like to visit? Why?*

*What might it be like to spend a day there, or to eat dinner with a kind family in that nation?

*What do you think they eat there? In your imagination, what does it taste like?

Why is that the nation you pictured? What makes your heart drawn to that place?

* What are 3 interesting things about the nation you chose?

1.

2.

3.

* What do you think the people are like in that nation? List 3 interesting things about the people and culture of that nation?

1.

2.

3.

* How is your "Dream" of what you hope to give to the world needed in that specific nation?

* Is there a big need in that nation that relates to your "Compassion?" Explain.

* How does your "Passion" fit in that nation? Is it common or popular there? Is there a big need for that profession or interest? Be creative in thinking about how you might use your passion.

* How is your "Purpose" used in that nation? Is it common? Is it needed? How could it fit for you there? Where is the opportunity?

* How can you study more about that nation to learn about its people, cultures, geography, government and needs? (Ex: internet, books, family, friends, teachers, mentors, etc.)

* Take the time to study the nation you chose and list 5 new things you learned.

1.

2.

3.

4.

5.

The more you learn does your heart grow bigger for that nation? How? Why?

* Based on what you learned, what might it look like to add more HOPE to that nation?

* Does focusing on that nation cause you to adjust your "Dream" or "Purpose" at all? If so, how?

What if you found a way, starting now, to give hope to even a few people in that nation? What are some possible ways you could do that without traveling there yet?

Imagine

Imagine you had nothing in your hands or wallet except one little seed. But, you decided to believe in that seed because you could see that deep down there was a tree that lived inside of it. It takes vision to see the tree inside a seed before it is formed; but it is there!

So, you took that seed and sent it to someone across the world. Imagine they planted your one seed and took good care of it. Then, years later your seed became a tree. Now, your seed was big enough to provide shade and fruit for many people. Your little seed now started to feed many people and change lives, families and the community. And it all happened because you took your one seed, *believed in it*, and freely gave it across the world with love.

What might that seed be for you? Where, who or how would you send it? Why?

What is the small beginning you can start with? Where and how can you give, send or plant that seed? Be creative. Instead of thinking about what you cannot do, dream about what you can do!

The game board and resources shown on the following pages is an activation we created based on what we have just walked through together.

It is meant to help you unlock the hope, purpose and dream that is already inside of you. We all have these areas inside of us, but often they are locked up, hidden, or lying buried and dormant. The goal of this is to help give you the freedom to unlock each of these areas in your heart, and then connect the dots to see how you are a living picture of hope, value and purpose. It is a visual of what we have been walking through in this section.

Putting It All Together

The "First Steps" after the "Nations" section is one that we already applied to each category. It is essentially to help you not just dream about it, but to find one or two first steps that you can actually take to get started. Often, it's those courageous first steps to start and put ourselves out there that go the furthest in making dreams and purpose come to life.

When you realize the "Dream" you want to give the world, and focus on your "Compassion," you can use your "Passion" to reach them through a unique "Purpose" suited to your gifts and talents. Choose from the "Nations" the place that grabs your heart and then put in place one or two "First Steps" to get started.

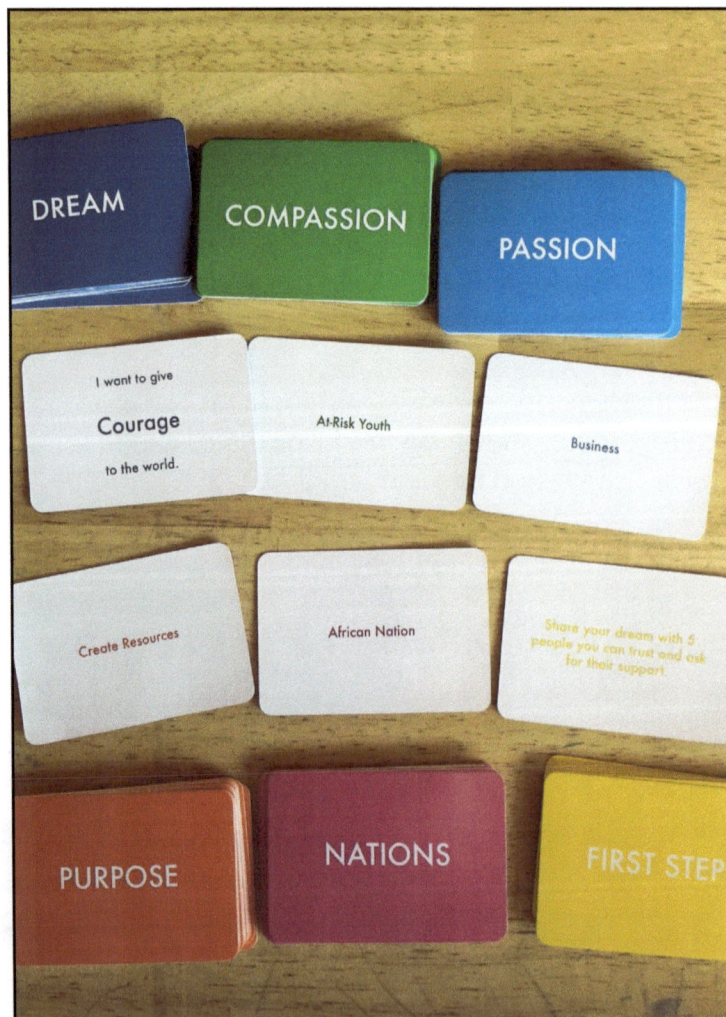

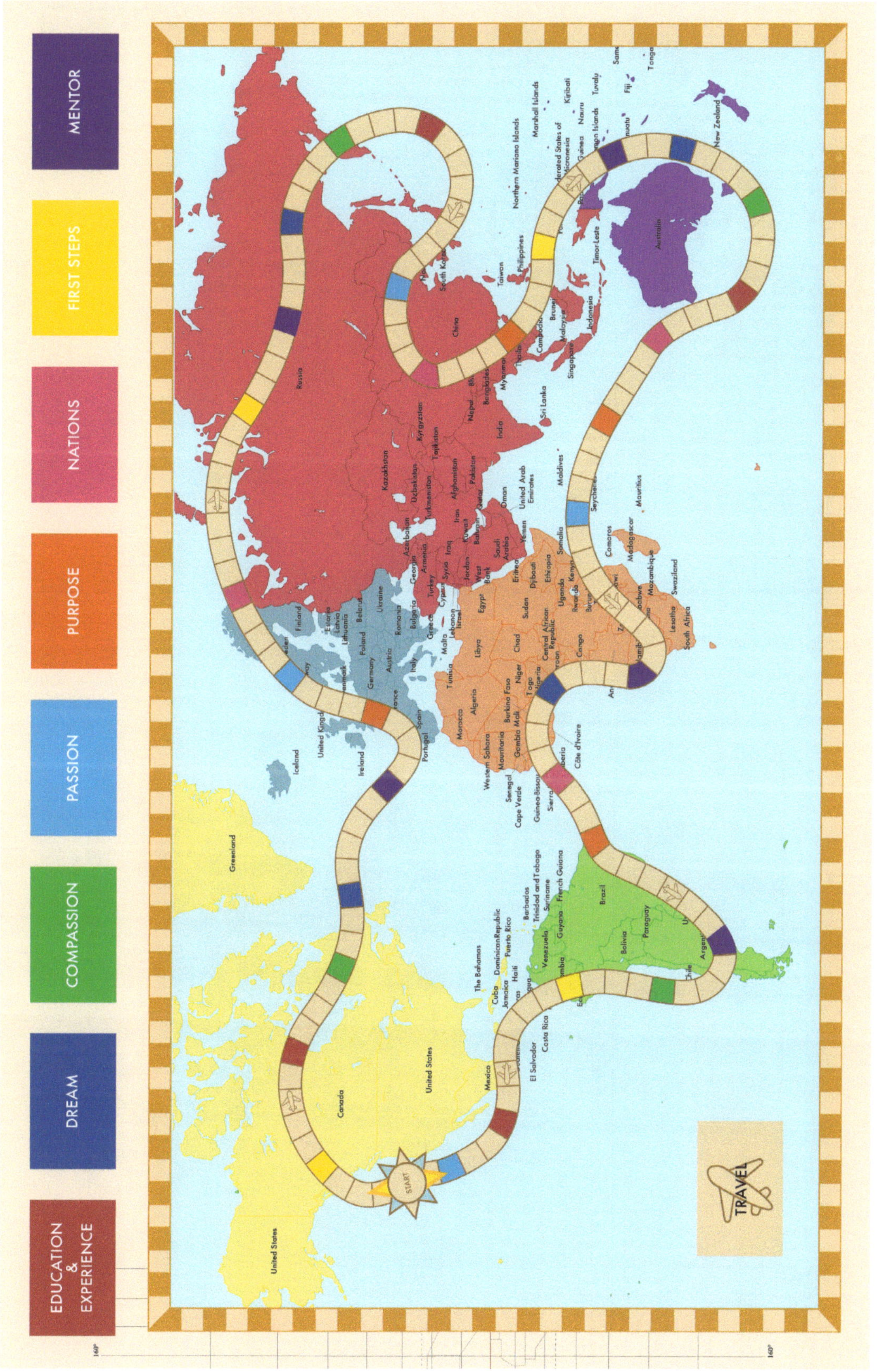

EDUCATION & EXPERIENCE
DREAM
COMPASSION
PASSION
PURPOSE
NATIONS
FIRST STEPS
MENTOR
START
TRAVEL
United States
Canada
Greenland
Iceland
Mexico
Brazil
Russia
China
India
Australia
New Zealand

(From the Mt. Shasta Herald, article/photo by Shareen Strauss)

(Empowering young leaders in the Middle East.)

Section Seven:
We Believe In You!

You were created to be an over-comer that rises above the pressures of the world to help others in their time of need.

What are we feeding ourselves?

Something interesting happens when a female bee is born. Every single one is born with the same genetic make up and opportunity. But then, that's where things start to change. See, after a female bee is born a decision is made. She is either sent to the smaller, more confined space and fed honey to grow, therefore becoming a normal worker bee. Or, others are sent to the larger space, with more room or higher ceilings if you will. These bees aren't just fed the normal stuff either; they're given royal jelly instead. These are the one's who *then* become Queen bees.

They weren't born a queen, rather, they have the same original construct as any of the others. However, there came a time where they were given something more than others. There came a time where they were fed like royalty, and therefore they became royalty.

Some reading this might look at it like those born into poverty vs. those born into wealth, and I can definitely see where you're coming from. But, there is more.

What this really should tell us is that there is still opportunity beyond what you are born into.

Because in our world, that decision doesn't just have to be made according to where you are born, or into what circumstances or what family situation you arrived. No, in our world we can be fed or choose to start feeding off the royal jelly at any time, and suddenly find ourselves beyond the limited confines we knew and starting to live into a more royal, or a more "purple" if you will, way of life.

The power of "belief" is greater than most of us know. This power is true when we believe in ourselves and daily learn to feed off of good things that strengthen that belief. And it is especially true when someone comes along, or when you come along for someone else, and give them your belief!

It's one of the most powerful acts in this world, *to believe*.

In this section it is important we learn to feed ourselves belief and courage to help us persevere in what can be a difficult world. And it will be life-changing—for you and others—if you learn how to believe in the people around you more often.

When we feel believed in, suddenly, anything seems possible and we overcome things that would have overcome us previously, and we persevere through circumstances we otherwise might use as an excuse to compromise. Belief gives us courage, and courage is an internal belief that doesn't deny fear, but courage does help us defy fear.

We cannot just fabricate that courage or "fake it" by taking on all comers; no, true courage starts with belief.

You or those around you may not have been born into bigger spaces being fed royal jelly, but you can choose what you feed yourself, and especially what you feed others! The decision of how we use our belief will alter the world as we know it.

Understanding & Embracing the Process

"You can have anything you want if you want it badly enough. You can be anything you want to be, do anything you set out to accomplish if you hold to that desire with singleness of purpose."   - Abraham Lincoln

There is a process to our purpose that cannot be ignored. The more we learn to embrace the process involved—rather than look for immediate results—the more chance we have of seeing our purpose fully realized.

Purpose's Path: The River

To live out our purpose, or even look at such from a high bird's eye view, our path throughout our journey would often look like that of a windy, forward moving river.

When you look at a river from overhead, or on a map, you see how it twists and turns left, then forward, then right, and so forth—and sometimes it even doubles back. The river's path is a series of steps forward, course corrections, downhill streams and even seasons of stillness. The river is the ultimate pioneer in that it is always moving forward, always taking new ground, and ALWAYS giving life (bearing fruit/results) wherever it goes.

But the pathway of the river, for us, is not always easy when we begin such a path expecting a paved racetrack to easy success. That is often the mindset we have come to expect and the mindset we unfortunately use to measure the success of our dreams. It is why so many people give up on their dreams and the hope and purpose within them, because it is harder than they expect, not always a straight, clean path forward, and often without the instant gratification they have been taught.

Purpose is definitely not the path of least resistance, but the river is a life-force that has resistance in itself. The river's inner resistance becomes greater than the resistance it faces, and therefore the river continues to carve out and take new ground to change the world around it.

Each of us, each of you, are created with the innate nature of a river. Two things can happen. When you meet resistance and don't see an easy road or immediate success you can stop and become more like a mini-pond of standing water. Or, you can embrace the process of the river, and let your resistance overcome that which you are facing. We know who you are and what you are capable of, but do you? You are a river, not a pond.

"The greatest thing in this world is not so much where we stand as in what direction we are moving."
                                                    - Johann Wolfgang von Goethe

Perseverance and Persistence

As just mentioned, a river has an inner resistance inside it that is bigger than it may realize. This helps the river persevere when it faces a difficult season of weather or hard, rocky ground. It is a river's nature to keep moving forward, to keep flowing. It has to work against its nature and its true identity not to persevere through that rocky ground or those frozen temperatures. As we have learned, the world has often taught us a wrong, counterfeit or lesser version of our true identity, so many of us don't know who we are or what we are capable of. The world has taught us to change our nature and settle for becoming a pond. However, you were created to persevere, and to overcome, it is inside of you the way moving water is within a river. Don't settle for the identity of a pond, but be the forward moving, forward thinking river you have been created to be.

-What is the difference between a river and a pond?

-How does a river's inner resistance help it overcome?

-What is perseverance or persistence?

-Why do we often conform our identity to be more like a pond instead of a river?

-Why do we need to embrace the process of a river?

-Which one do you want to be? Why?

Patience & Timing

A river does not just embrace patience for the sake of patience alone. Patience is part of a bigger picture called "timing" or "seasons." Many things only happen in the right season. You can hope the leaves turn colors and fall off in spring but that hope probably won't be realized. You can try to plant in fall and harvest in winter, but that doesn't usually work. You can try to take a summer break from school in February but you're not likely to be excused. Likewise, certain fruits, flowers and more only grow at specific times each year. When we learn to embrace those correct times and seasons we find much better results.

To find the right season for summer break, you have to go through the process of the school year first. To grow an apple you have to plant a seed, nourish a root, and wait for a tree and its branches first. To every worthwhile result there is a process that must be taken step-by-step to get there.

One of the strengths of the river is that it knows how to navigate each season without stopping, nor changing whom it is to fit in or try and find external peace. A river passes through summer days peacefully; it navigates the changes of fall, the freezing temperatures of winter, and the rushing rapids of spring. All the while, it is still a river that keeps moving forward, patiently embracing the best parts of each season of its process.

The more we learn to embrace that different seasons of our lives are for different parts of the process, the happier we will be while we persevere forward. We won't be expecting apples before they're ready, or hope to go skiing in July. Your purpose will have a process, and you will find new challenges and new rewards in each season while you work towards your goal. Keep moving forward in your purpose and dream, because there is hope in every season.

-*Why is patience important?*

-*Why is correct timing important?*

-*How does patience partner with "timing"?*

-*Why don't apples grow directly from seeds? What is the process in between?*

-*Do you think your purpose or dream might have a similar path as the process in between a seed and an apple?*

-*How can you learn to embrace that process?*

-Why is every season important?

-How do you keep moving forward through every season?

-Is embracing process worth it? Why?

Adjustment

Even though you persevere towards a specific hope or vision, the middle and the end won't always look like what you pictured at first. This is not just okay, but it is a good thing! Your hope and vision will grow and change because you are continuing to grow. It might have a lot of the same DNA or life that you dreamed of from the beginning, but maybe in a different form, or maybe the way it will come to life will surprise you. Because of this, on our journey of purpose we need to learn to leave room for adjustment; it is one of the most powerful things we can learn. Did you know you can adjust without changing? That's exactly what a river does.

A river is still itself, still has the same goal, and is still moving forward. But sometimes it has to change course a little for various reasons. Sometimes the river runs into a mountain and needs to swerve left in order to persevere. Sometimes a river needs to be more still and move slowly because of the freezing temperatures of winter. Does this mean the river failed or made a mistake and is being punished? Of course not, winter is a natural thing for a river to pass through. It just needs to adjust and keep moving forward. Sometimes a river needs to turn right to pick up some seeds and nutrients before it turns back again to carry those seeds and nutrients to a place that needs them badly. But even through these kinds of adjustments, the river is always moving forward, always taking ground, and always carrying life to change the world wherever it goes.

It's not always about the end goal, but how we carry ourselves during the in between times. Sometimes our adjustments to the right or left, or doubling back for one reason or another are more important than the destination. When we learn to embrace those parts of the process and learn and grow from them, it will only add to the life that's in our water and we'll have even more impact on the people and world around us as we move forward.

-What is one reason why adjustment can be important for a river?

-What is another example of why a river needs to adjust?

-Why is adjustment important for you to learn?

-How can adjustment help your purpose?

-Is the need for adjustment a punishment? Why not?

-What do we need to do during adjustment?

-How do you learn and grow during those times?

-Will your purpose and dream be greater from learning to adjust, learn and grow? How?

-How will you embrace adjustment as part of the process? Give some possible examples that relate to you and your dream?

Differing Results

A river produces very different results than a pond. With a pond, it seems much simpler to measure results and see them right away. Because a pond is stagnant, standing water it is easier to measure its impact. It is easier to count how many fish the pond has, how many trees it calls its own, how much water it has, how big it is, etc. But the pond has all these results at the expense of one really important thing: the pond, because it is stagnant, standing water, grows more fungus and disease that also pollutes the nature of its water. So, with a pond, you may get more measurable results around your water, but your water itself starts to suffer.

A river is not nearly as measurable in the results department. It is always moving, always turning; it crosses territories, not sure who it belongs to or how many fish or trees belong to itself. This is true because it is always moving forward, and it's that forward movement that keeps its waters pure. And the reality is that a river has far many more trees with far more fruit than the pond has, it is just more difficult to measure because its boundaries are harder to define and said trees and fruit is more spread out.

The river probably has far more fish as well, but they are swimming place to place, moving up and down the river and hard to count because the river doesn't just house the fish, it leads them forward as well.

The river carries nutrients wherever it goes inside that moving, living water that births grass, and bushes, trees and fruit. But the river doesn't always see those results because it is moving forward to give life in its next step. See, for the river, it's not about what results can be measured to its name, it's about the impact it makes, the ground it takes and the life it gives wherever it goes while continuing to live its truest identity through all seasons.

Our purposes and dreams are not unlike the river in this way either. Our dreams and the purpose within them aren't necessarily supposed to be about the result we have or the recognition we receive. Moving forward in our purposes and dreams are more about the life-giving impact we make as we continue to be who we were created to be, embrace or process, and keep moving forward with hope.

-How are results measured around a pond?

-Why are results harder to measure for the river?

-Why does a river have more pure water as it moves forward?

-What kind of results does a river produce?

-Why should our life and purpose be more like a river in this way?

-What should be the greatest results of our process and purpose? How?

-How can you be more like a river than a pond in this way?

Failure Is Not What It Seems

"Keep moving forward." – Walt Disney

The above quote by Walt Disney is one that I use frequently, mostly because it is not just a quote but should be a way of life and the posture of our heart. My heart has learned what it means to persevere because it always sees that hope is alive. We keep moving forward beyond the failures or setbacks of the moment because we know that hope is still inside us, and we see where and for what purpose that hope needs to go. We can't give up on our mission to take our seed of hope and plant it in the fields of our destiny—for that is where and when it will shine brightest and give life to the most people. We must come to a point where failure is not "failure" as we have come to know it, rather, failure is just one of many stepping stones we leap from that helps us grow, navigate obstacles and move forward to pioneer our unique purpose in the world. Below are some great examples of those who failed at first, persevered, and later had great success.

"I haven't failed. I've just found 10,000 ways that won't work." - Thomas Edison

Albert Einstein:

- *Early Failure:* He wasn't able to speak until he was nearly 4 years old and his teachers said he *"would never amount to much."*

- **Later Success:** Became a world famous Theoretical Physicist & Nobel Prize Winner.

Michael Jordan:

- *Early Failure:* After being cut from his high school basketball team he went home, locked himself in his room, and cried.

- **Later Success:** 6 Time NBA World Champion, 5 Time NBA Most Valuable Player.

Oprah Winfrey:

- **_Early Failure:_** _Was demoted from her news anchor job because they said she was "not fit for television."_

- **Later Success:** Host of multi-award winning T.V. talk show and name "The Most Influential Woman in the World."

Steve Jobs:

- **_Early Failure:_** _At 30 he was devastated and depressed after being unceremoniously removed from the company he started._

- **Later Success:** Co-founder of Apple, Co-founder of Pixar Animation Studio

Walt Disney:

- **_Early Failure:_** _Was fired from a newspaper job for "lacking imagination" and having "no original ideas."_

- **Later Success:** Creator of Disney, Mickey Mouse, and winner of 22 Academy Awards.

Lionel Messi:

- **_Early Failure:_** _At age 11 he was cut from his futbol/soccer team after being diagnosed with a growth hormone deficiency, which made him smaller in stature than most kids his age._

- **Later Success:** 3 Time FIFA World Player of the Year

Thomas Edison:

- ***Early Failure:*** *A teacher told him he was "too stupid to learn anything" and that "he should go into a field where he might succeed by virtue of his pleasant personality" instead.*

- **Later Success:** Inventor of the light bulb

We must learn—*and remember*—that failure is not something to be afraid or ashamed of. It is not final. Failure is not who you are and does not define you. The hope and possibility in you is much greater, and like these amazing examples, that hope and possibility is waiting to be lived out through you with great purpose and impact. Have the courage to try, and fail, and the courage to try again!

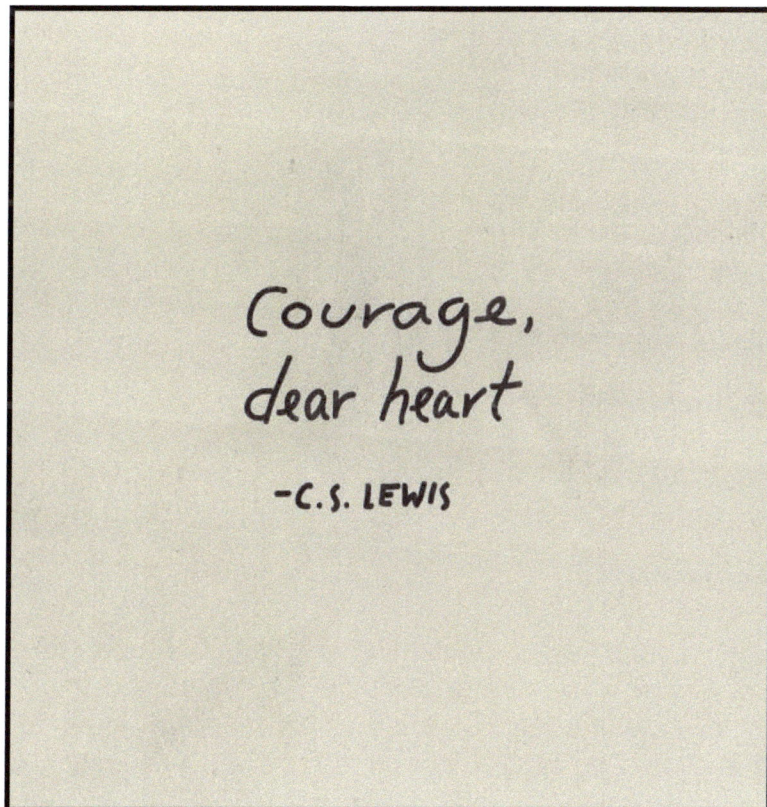

Courage,
dear heart

-C.S. LEWIS

Courage to "Keep Moving Forward":

We'll leave you with this following section to help strengthen and encourage your steps forward. We all face opposition at times, and we all need to remember the truth that helps us persevere. The following section is from a resource we've produced to give to those we're working with so that way they have daily reminders to go over as they start their journey forward.

We will list each one for the possibility of discussion to help you understand how each of these might apply during various steps or challenges of your journey. They are great reminders of much of what we have covered thus far, and are here to help you to "keep moving forward" even when things get tough.

"Courage Cards"

"Today is a new opportunity to start living your purpose. Start with 1 new step."

> - Any given day is a new opportunity. Sometimes it is in the most challenging circumstances that we have to arise with hope, and when it feels the hardest take just ONE new step forward. That one step tells our circumstances that we will not allow difficulties to weigh down or control our life. That one step can prove that our hope is bigger.

"You will be encouraged as you encourage others. Who can you encourage today?"

> - To encourage someone else we first have to take our eyes off of self, which helps us not to fall further into negative thoughts. When we do this, and give hope to someone else, it naturally encourages us too. It's the times when we don't feel much hope at all that we can re-start hope in our lives by first giving it to others.

"Thankfulness will help lead you forward. Even if your dreams aren't working out yet, keep finding people and reasons to be thankful for."

- I once read of a person in the midst of a terrible time in life. Suddenly they were reminded of this powerful truth, "Try giving thanks." When discouragement wants to push us down it is an attitude of thankfulness that helps lift our spirits higher. Instead of focusing on or counting all that is wrong, an attitude of thankfulness counts and highlights all that is good, has been good, or that which could be great!

"Keep your hope alive! Don't let anything or anyone steal your hope. Hope will help you see clearly to keep moving forward."

- Your hope is a buoy to your heart. Hope gives you vision for possibility, for change, for good. This is the kind of vision we need most when times get tough. Hope is like the most expensive, wonderful, important pair of glasses or sunglasses that you've ever owned. Protect them, don't forget about them in your pocket, and keep wearing them!

"You have been created for amazing purposes and plans. The hard things in your life are not who you are, they are what you will overcome."

- Never forget that you have a purpose—a great purpose! Challenges and difficulties will only help prove your purpose, and give you an opportunity to rise up and live that purpose. Don't waste your challenges, they are there to help prove who you were and are created to be.

"Don't let your eyes drift to start looking at yourself or your circumstances, you must keep looking up, and looking forward. There are great possibilities ahead!"

- Circumstances try and get us to hang our head in discouragement. Notice that when you hang your head you are looking down and can't see the vision of hope for your life. We rarely find many hopeful answers while looking down. You might not always be able to change your circumstances, but you can always fight for where you keep your focus.

"Take time to remember the good and great things that have happened to you, there is more than you think."

- Similar to thankfulness, it's important to take time to look back over the good memories and milestones in our lives. We often take too much time thinking backwards about failures or other difficulties. If we are going to look back, why not use that time to look back in a good way. Those good memories and milestones will remind you how you persevered, how you overcame, and will show you how far you have come up to this point. Those good memories will help set you up to take even bigger leaps forward in the future!

"Love is the strongest force in the world. Remember, you are loved and created to show love to others. Love will change the world."

- The world tries to tempt us to pick up things like bitterness, hatred or un-forgiveness—as if those will help us. They hurt us more than they do the people we hold them towards. They are unseen, silent poisons in our soul. Love is always the medicine. Love has to be the filter we pass everything through as it will be the quickest way to keep hope, and give hope. It can be hard, but if you choose love each time you will never have a regret.

"Don't compare yourself to others; it will only rob your joy. Remember the passion and joy in your heart and the purpose YOU have been created for."

- Comparing yourself to another is like being specially chosen to play the guitar but instead of playing we keep looking over our shoulder to compare ourselves to the drummer and the different music they are playing. They are supposed to be using a different instrument, and playing their music differently. And so are you! Keep looking forward, keep playing the music you were created to play and enjoy! Where would the band be without a guitarist?

"You can't always control what happens to you, but you can control how you respond to what happens. You can change your circumstances with your attitude and your response."

- There are a lot of things, and people, that we can't control in life. That is something we have to accept. But we don't ever have to accept a bad attitude or a lack of hope. The fastest way to bring hopeful change to someone or something else is to live that change in our lives first. Your attitude, choices and the way you respond will always be the greatest example you have to give and no one can take that away from you if you don't let them.

"Patience often feels difficult, but with your belief and courage, patience might be the very thing that brings to life your purpose and dream."

- There is an old saying that "good things come to those who wait." We still need to move forward, we still need to take action, but we must have patience while we do. It is great wisdom to know when to be patient. Practice that. Patience is often the best partner to hope and action. It can be kind of like walking. Your right foot is Action, your left foot represents Patience. They have to work together in order to move forward.

"Bigger things are happening than what you can see. Even if you don't see the results yet, remember, plants grow roots underground first before they give life in front of your eyes."

- It is important to remember that our physical eyes don't always tell us the whole story. Sometimes we have to do what we know is right, and trust that over time that right choice or step will produce good fruit.

"Like a tree, you have to nourish and nurture the root of your dreams before you can share its fruit with the world. Stay true in the small things and you can trust big blessings will follow too."

- We usually like picking fruit or eating the fruit of a tree more than we like watering it with nothing to show—yet! But great, enjoyable, and hopeful results don't come without many small, faithful steps. Have integrity in the small choices, they add up to great things over time. You won't be sorry.

"No matter what you have been through, there is always hope! Keep believing—you are not alone."

- It's easy to lose hope, but harder to get it back. Don't let go of your hope! No matter what you are facing, face it with hope. Even when you feel alone in the direction or purpose you are going, there are people around you who care about you and believe in you. You may not see them at this moment, but they are there. You can always step out of the moment and gain a bigger perspective so that your feelings don't make your decision for you.

"You might have to take a bold step into unknown territory to discover treasures that others haven't found yet. It can feel like blind faith, but that is often what is needed to see the special purposes you were created for come to life."

- Few people have found great treasures without going where others hadn't gone, or wouldn't go. No one has lived your unique purpose before, so it will take faith to keep stepping into unknown territory. There's a famous quote that says, "If you always do what you have always done, you will always get what you have always gotten." Your results usually won't change for the better without a new and better step to begin.

"Sometimes trying to live your dream and purpose can feel like walking on water; like you are sinking and don't know where to put your foot next. Don't look at the water, look at your goal. Keep stepping forward and trusting the one who created you for such special purpose."

- Walking out our purpose in life doesn't always feel very steady, often with worries on either side of us like waves trying to knock us down. But don't give in to the worry or fear. Keep walking forward one step at a time. And as we have talked about, keep looking up so you can keep seeing HOPE! The waves and water of your circumstances will rarely send you the right direction, but will try and get you to sink. But you weren't created with a purpose to sink, you were created with a purpose to overcome, to shine, and help bring hope to the world.

"You have value inside that can be given away to others without losing it yourself. As you freely give to others, you will find that you freely receive as well."

- Oftentimes we do not give because we think giving to others will create lack for us. But actually, the opposite is true. Remember, we are not supposed to be living by a value system of "money," but a measurement system of genuine value, like "gold." When we give freely to others to benefit them it doesn't create a deficit in us, but it takes what we give and multiplies it because we are investing in hope and the value we see in other people. We receive great value by giving, and they receive great value from receiving—double value.

"Take time to journal the steps you have taken, the positive things that have happened so far, and what you have learned. All of such will help you in your next steps."

- Journaling is a very helpful exercise because it helps you remember, and process, where you have been and where you hope to be going. It is a written map of your journey. It can also be a friend to help you process some of the inner thoughts and feelings you are having, getting them out on paper into the light which keeps them from weighing you down on the inside.

"No true dream comes to life without patience and perseverance. If you are having to fight to keep your dream alive, you're probably on the right path."

- Your dream would not be a true "dream" if it were easy. Perseverance through obstacles and challenging circumstances actually helps produce more hope. Every obstacle you overcome reminds you and others of what is possible.

"You are incredibly valuable just for WHO you are. You carry something special into every room you enter and to every person you encounter or spend time with."

- Remember, there is gold in you that the world needs to know. The world will not value you if you do not learn to value yourself. Just as gold shines and reflects light, so do you. Do not ever walk into a room without knowing that you have something special to offer just by being you. People might not say it often enough, but they are impacted by who you are.

"Sometimes it is hard to stand up for the right thing, but your courage to do what is right even when you feel pressured is noticed and felt more than you know. Your courage to keep believing changes the world."

- Every time you stand up against the wrong pressures of the world or from other people and make the right decision you make a difference in the world. Your right choices and example are noticed and felt, even if others won't say it at first. It takes more courage to do the right thing than to give in to the wrong thing.

"As you show mercy and kindness to others, you plant seeds of life that can never be uprooted. Love never fails!"

- When you give love or random acts of kindness to others you won't always see the difference immediately, but that is okay because we don't give just so we can receive. Instead, we become like someone who plants a seed in the desert every day and returns there 5 years later to find it is no longer a desert, but is flourishing with beautiful flowers and growing trees. Sometimes the greatest change will happen one seed at a time over a long period of time. Your love, kindness and mercy towards others are those seeds.

"Don't allow your youth to hold you back; you can start living your purpose today. There are people around you who need your youthful hope, courage and belief."

- There are parts of your purpose that will come later in life, but there is also a great and needed light in you that needs to shine now! Some of the greatest world changers this earth has ever seen have been those who chose to live for hope and purpose at a young age. It doesn't mean you have all the answers, but it does mean you have something important to contribute. Spend time with mentors who will support you and believe in you to live this out.

"Love is the only weapon you'll ever need for those who have or will hurt you. Use your courage to show love even when others do not. Love always wins!"

- When you turn the other cheek and refuse to return hurt for hurt, you demonstrate not that you are too weak to react but that you are strong enough to believe in something greater. It takes courage to show love towards those who hurt us, but that love proves the hope that is building and growing within us. A wise man named Ghandi once said, *"An eye for an eye will make the whole world blind."* We need to be the one who breaks that cycle. Instead of adding to the blindness of the world, our attitudes and acts of love and mercy can instead be what gives the world back its true vision!

"Don't hide your light today. Remember, the darkness and pressures of the world that try and bully you is more afraid of you and the light you were created to shine."

- Fear, insecurity and darkness are just bullies who use pressure. Most bullies act big and tough on the outside because they are so insecure and fearful on the inside. Similarly, fear and insecurity are actually much more afraid of the powerful hope they know are inside of you. Don't let those pressures cause you to hide your light. Your light is not only needed in your life, but in the lives all around you. And if you keep your light on, it might help someone else keep theirs on too.

"Keep hope alive, and it will be a bridge to walk into the destiny you were created for."

- It's hard to walk across a canyon to your destination on the other side if there is no bridge. And it's also nearly as difficult to walk across on a broken bridge. Hope is your bridge. Every time you are struggling to step into your purpose or your destiny, do something to give your hope a boost! Your hope will strengthen the bridge and make your current path better, and more possible. The bridge starts on the inside before you walk on it on the outside.

"Empower others the same way you wish to be empowered. There are others all around you who might not say it, but they are waiting for someone to believe in them."

- When we learn to give others what we want, we take away the power that selfishness or jealously can try and have in our lives. When we empower someone it is like starting a game of Leap Frog. In the game of Leap Frog you can only go forward by jumping over someone. But after you let them jump over you, they get down and let you jump over them so that you can keep moving forward together. As you believe in them and help them move forward, they, and others, will do the same for you.

"When you over think, you start to sink. If you feel discouraged, find a way to take your eyes off of yourself by serving someone else nearby."

- Over thinking your challenges suddenly becomes like quicksand in your mind. The more you think about the negative the faster that quicksand sucks you down into the pits and it is even harder to get out of the pit once you are down there. Instead, stop the quicksand of negative thoughts when they start, recognizing that the only place they will take you is down. Look for someone to help or encourage and take your eyes off of your negative circumstances. Your hope will get renewed in the process of helping them.

"The values you live by are worth far more than the money or things you have in your hands. Show the world today what true value looks like by the way you live."

- When you know the "golden" identity you have inside you, you will take care of and value that gold in a different way. You will make wise decisions and use it in positive ways. The world sees and feels this. Live from the value you have on the inside rather than what you don't have on the outside.

"You were created to be an over-comer who rises above the pressures of the world to help others in their time of need."

- The world needs more people like you. It needs more people who refuse to let hope die, who persevere, and who overcome the pressures all around. You were created to live the life of an overcomer, and as you live that life your example and your attitude will multiply to others who are watching all around you. Stay true to your overcoming heart!

"Did you know, when there is a storm, an eagle actually rises higher and flies towards or above the storm? They were created to rise higher in difficult moments—so are you!"

- I love this example! An eagle was actually created to rise above difficulties and conquer the storms in its life. The eagle is the ultimate picture of a leader who has vision and hope from a higher perspective. We should all live more like the eagle in that way.

"Live by faith, hope and love. But remember, the greatest is love."

- Your hope and your belief are two of the most powerful things you have to keep moving forward by. But, they are still no match for the love you have inside you. Love is at the center of the gold you have inside you. When you choose to live and respond in genuine, selfless love, you prove and show the value of the gold inside you.

"If there are any negative words in your head about yourself, write them down to expose them as lies. Then, tear them up to remind yourself they do not exist. Lies are only as true as you allow them to be. Your life was created for truth."

- We can all battle different negative thoughts or lies in our head. The important thing is not to believe them or live as if they're true. It helps to get the lies out into the light of day and see them somewhere other than the solitude of our mind. When the light hits those lies it exposes them for the lies they are and helps us return to a truthful perspective about ourselves and others.

"Repeat this out loud: I am valued, I am loved, I have purpose, I am believed in! Repeat it again!"

- This is one that might be worth repeating out loud every day. When we don't have someone else there that day to give us this pep talk, it's important to remind ourselves. There are enough negative thoughts we have to fight against each day, so we should take time to plant true and hopeful words into ourselves instead. You are worth it!

"Love is your foundation, your platform to make a difference from, and the stage from which you sing."

- If we are living out of our true "golden" identity, we will not be living FOR an identity, but we will be living FROM our identity. The difference is that if we are living FOR an identity we are looking for any stage anywhere we can find to be seen. But to live FROM our identity is to know that we are loved for who we were created to be and stand and live on that stage every day. We shouldn't have to go looking for something that is less than what we already have.

"True courage is to be faithful even when no one is looking. Those are the moments that will be part of the foundation of living your purpose and dream!"

- Again, we are talking about the courage to live from the inside out, and the integrity to do so all the time, not just because it gets us something but because we believe it is the right way. Each time you have the courage to make a right—and sometimes difficult—choice, you take a step further into fulfilling your special and hopeful purpose in this world. Keep stepping forward, and keep doing so with true courage. We believe in you!

Champions Exercise

No matter who you are, where you come from, or whether or not you feel you have someone believing in you yet—we can still start to believe in others. I want to challenge you to pick one person in your relative sphere of influence, whether they are in your family, your neighborhood, your school, workplace or other; and for the next month I want to challenge you to "Champion" them.

Look for ways, both verbal, written or through actions that convey to them that you believe in them. Let them hear it, see it and feel it—but don't tell them what you're doing—*show them*! Watch what happens in their life during that month. Pay attention to how it strengthens them, how it picks up their spirits and even how it affects their decisions. Your consistent belief can change their life, give them renewed hope, and help their ability to believe in their own value and purpose.

Find someone to champion!

Pioneering Purpose

"Hope deferred makes the heart grow sick, but a desire fulfilled is a tree of life." – King Solomon

I like the "but" in the middle of this quote. Many focus on and live in the hope-deferred part for their whole life. But this whole journey together has been about transitioning through that *"but…"* It leads us to the truth that when a desire is actually fulfilled, you and that dream become a tree of life that keeps bearing fruit and giving life to others beyond what you even know. And often, the only difference between staying in hope deferred and moving into a desire fulfilled, is the choice of how you see yourself, how you believe, how you persevere in hope, and how you freely give to and empower others. Keep moving forward!

From this day on, leave behind all that has stolen your hope and made you heartsick. Instead, step forward into a life of hope, of vision, of identity and worth. Step with courage, backed by love and belief into a life of dreams fulfilled and purpose engaged. You carry something special just by being you, and you have something to give that someone, somewhere in the world is waiting for. Now is the time to start. **We believe in you!** Now is the time for you to believe, too.

Anything is possible. But we won't scratch the surface if we don't empower one another with value, love, purpose and belief.

(Here is Alex 10 years later as he continues the legacy of empowering others, long after we left.)